Eat Well,

Jamie

Inspired Ideas For Entertaining

Bountiful Buffets

JAMIE GWEN with Lana Sills

Published by:
Tastebud Entertainment, Inc.
Los Angeles, CA

Chef Jamie® is licensed by Tastebud Ent., Inc.

Food Styling by Lana Sills and Jamie Gwen
Food Photography by Bob Hodson Photography

Printed in the USA

We have worked and entertained together for many years and we have always been great collaborators....so first and foremost we acknowledge each others loving dedication and passion for food.

This book is devoted to our enthusiastically hungry friends, who have allowed us to bask in what we love! Thank you for enjoying our weekday celebrations, our weekend soirees, our last-minute invites and our love for everyday entertaining...Without you to eat it all, we would never move on to new recipes!

And to you, the reader and fabulous foodie, thank you for adding this book to your collection, for being inspired to entertain with bountiful buffets and for creating new memories with our favorite recipes.

Jamie Gwen and Lana Sills

CONTENTS

~~~

PERFECT
SOLUTIONS
for EVERYDAY
BUFFETS

PERFECT SOLUTIONS for EVERYDAY BUFFETS

A Beautiful Brunch
White Wine Poached Eggs
Citrus Chive Hollandaise Sauce
Apple Glazed Sausages
A Basket of Freshly Baked Muffins and Scones
Peach Bellinis or Mango Mimosas

Cocktails and Hors D'Oeuvres
Warm Blue Cheese Dip with Homemade Potato Chips
Sweet & Spicy Cashews
Spicy Roasted Olives
Creamy Chipotle Hummus
Pomegranate Martinis

A Warm and Welcoming Soup Buffet
Corn and Crab Chowder
French Onion Soup
Creamy Vegetable Chowder
Lemony Caesar Salad
Cornbread with Honey Butter
Rosemary Breadsticks

Sunday Supper
Individual Meatloaves with Pan Gravy
Bacon Mac and Cheese
Sautéed Green Beans
Butterscotch Pudding

Dinner with Friends
Red Wine Mushroom Ragout on French Bread Toasts
Pesto and Cheese-Filled Chicken Breasts
Caramelized Shallots, Parsnips and Potatoes

Game Day Buffet
Maple Glazed Chicken Wings
Sweet and Sour Meatballs
Spicy Vegetarian Chili
The Ultimate Bittersweet Hot Fudge Sauce over Brownies and Ice Cream

PERFECT SOLUTIONS for EVERYDAY BUFFETS

Effortless and Impressive
Sautéed Chicken with Riesling and Mushrooms
Glazed Root Vegetables with Lemon and Honey
Tomato, Mozzarella and Basil Salad
Riesling and Pinot Noir

A Ladies Lunch
Chicken Bruschetta
Cauliflower Gratin
Salad of Arugula and Shaved Fennel with a Lemon Vinaigrette
Biscotti Stuffed Baked Apples

An All-Out Saturday Night Bash
Braised Lamb Shanks in Red Wine
Creamy Polenta with Crumbled Blue Cheese
Roasted Asparagus
Southern Bread Pudding with Brandy Sauce

Pasta Perfect
Fusilli with Bacon, Mushrooms, Asparagus and Cherry Tomatoes
Baked Ziti with Chicken Sausage and Three Cheeses
Fettuccini Gorgonzola
Toasted Garlic Bread
A Good Bottle of Chianti

Vegetarian Delight
Asparagus Risotto
Layers and Layers of Eggplant, Tomato and Mozzarella
Spicy Vegetarian Chili
Herbed Monkey Bread

An Outdoor Summer Affair
Raspberry Marinated Baked Chicken
Warm Antipasto Pasta Salad
Spicy Parmesan Corn on the Cob
Summer Peach Cobbler

PERFECT SOLUTIONS for EVERYDAY BUFFETS

Summer Memories
Baby Back Ribs with Espresso Barbecue Sauce
Asian Turkey Burgers
Warm Lemon Herb Potato Salad
Creamy Cole Slaw
Meyer Lemon Lemonade

Fondues for Friends
Classic Cheese Fondue
Apple Cider Cheddar Fondue
Fudge Fondue
Bread Cubes, Vegetables and Cooked Sausages for dipping
Chardonnay or Chateauneuf-du-Pape

Wedding Bliss
Apple Stuffed Pork Loin with Apple Shallot Cream Sauce
Chicken with Apricots, Figs and Olives
Classic Beef Stroganoff
Garlic Roasted Red Potatoes and Fennel
Nutty Rice Pilaf
Cauliflower Gratin

A Holiday Party Buffet
Traditional English Roast Beef
Spicy Sweet Potato Gratin
Brussels Sprouts with Bacon and Shallots

A Celebration of Dessert – The Perfect Ending
An Ice Cream Sundae Bar Buffet filled with…
Cherries Jubilee
Bananas Foster with Vanilla Ice Cream
The Ultimate Bittersweet Chocolate Sauce

A Brunch Buffet

Baked Eggs on a Bed of Sautéed Mushrooms

Scrambled Eggs Three Ways

White Wine Poached Eggs

Citrus Chive Hollandaise Sauce

Garden Frittata

Eggnog French Toast

Lemon Ricotta Pancakes
with Blueberry Maple Syrup

Apple Glazed Sausages

BAKED EGGS on a BED OF SAUTÉED MUSHROOMS

Serves 4

intro

Baked eggs are the perfect solution for a brunch crowd, a romantic breakfast, or for an elegant after-theater bite with champagne. You can bake eggs over all kinds of delicious things: bread, summer tomatoes, sautéed peppers, ratatouille, sautéed spinach and more. The perfect accompaniment to baked eggs? Champagne, of course!

ingredients

4 tablespoons unsalted butter
6 slices bread, cut into small cubes
2 tablespoons extra virgin olive oil
1/3 cup finely diced shallot or onion
1 pound baby portabella or cremini mushrooms, sliced
3 tablespoons freshly chopped parsley
3 teaspoons freshly chopped rosemary
Sea salt and freshly ground pepper
1 cup dry white wine
8 eggs
1/4 cup Parmesan Cheese

method

Preheat the oven to broil and set the rack about 4 to 5-inches from the heat. Lightly butter a baking dish.

Melt half the butter in a sauté pan and add the bread. Cook over low heat, stirring frequently, until golden and crisp, about 8 to 10 minutes. Divide the croutons between the two dishes.

Heat the oil and remaining butter in a sauté pan over medium heat. Add the shallot and sauté 3 minutes. Raise the heat and add the mushrooms. Sauté until the mushrooms have started to brown, about 5 minutes. Stir in the herbs and season with salt and pepper. Add the wine and scrape the pan to release the caramelized bits at the bottom of the pan. Lower the heat and simmer until almost dry. Season with salt and pepper and spoon the mushrooms into the baking dish.

Make eight tablespoon-size wells in the mushrooms and break the eggs into the wells. Season the eggs with salt and pepper and sprinkle 1 teaspoon of the Parmesan cheese over the top. Place the baking dish under the broiler. Broil the eggs until the whites are set and the yolks are still soft, about 4 to 5 minutes. Carefully remove the baked eggs from the oven and serve immediately.

SCRAMBLED EGGS THREE WAYS

Scrambled eggs are a chameleon—they can be adapted to the flavors of any cuisine around the world. Try these scrambled egg dishes at your next brunch. They are beautiful, flavorful and all of them are no-fail favorites for entertaining.

SCRAMBLED EGGS WITH CHILIES and QUESO

Serves 4

intro

This scrambled egg dish can be a fusion of Spanish and Greek flavors—with chilies and feta cheese—or the classic, south-of-the-border dish we love. Queso fresco is a fresh Mexican cheese, easily found in the refrigerated cheeses or specialty foods section of your market. Serve this scramble with warm flour tortillas and a garnish of chopped cilantro.

ingredients

4 tablespoons unsalted butter
2 tablespoons olive oil
1 small yellow onion, diced
1 large tomato, seeded and chopped
2 large poblano chilies, roasted (to remove the skins), seeded and diced
    or 4 ounces canned chopped green chilies
1/2 cup chopped green onions
2 garlic cloves, minced
8 large eggs, beaten
1 cup crumbled queso fresco or feta cheese
1/4 cup freshly chopped cilantro

method

Melt 2 tablespoons of the butter with the oil in large nonstick skillet over medium heat. Add the onion and chilies and sauté until the onion and chilies are tender, stirring often, about 10 minutes. Add the tomatoes and green onions and sauté 3 minutes more to meld the flavors. Add the garlic and sauté one minute more. Season with salt and pepper.

Add the remaining 2 tablespoons of butter to the pan over medium heat. Add the beaten eggs and the cheese. Cook until the eggs are softly set, stirring occasionally, about 4 minutes. Serve garnished with cilantro.

SCRAMBLED EGGS THREE WAYS

SCRAMBLED EGGS with TOMATO, BASIL and GOAT CHEESE

Serves 4

intro

I like to serve this "Italian scramble" with toasted flat bread and a side of fresh berries with yogurt, for a beautiful and satisfying brunch.

ingredients

3 tablespoons unsalted butter
2 shallots, chopped
1 large tomato, seeded, chopped
1/4 cup chopped green onions
8 large eggs, beaten
1/4 cup crumbled soft fresh goat cheese
1/4 cup freshly chopped basil
Salt and freshly ground pepper

method

Melt the butter in a large nonstick skillet over medium heat. Add the shallots and sauté 3 minutes. Add the chopped tomato and green onions and sauté 1 minute more. Season with salt and pepper. Add the beaten eggs, goat cheese and basil and cook until the eggs are softly set, stirring occasionally, about 4 minutes.

SCRAMBLED EGGS THREE WAYS

SCRAMBLED EGGS with SMOKED SALMON and CHIVES

Serves 4

intro

Smoked salmon elevates any meal to a special occasion. Fresh chopped chives and a dash of cream add a savory richness to this dish. Serve a side of twice-baked potatoes with a dollop of crème fraiche and a spoonful of caviar on top. Freshly squeezed orange or tangerine juice is a great, tart pairing with these intense flavors.

ingredients

8 large eggs
2 tablespoons heavy cream or Half & Half
4 tablespoons chopped fresh chives
3 tablespoons unsalted butter
3 shallots, minced
6 ounces thinly sliced smoked salmon, cut into strips
Salt and ground white pepper

method

Beat the eggs with the cream, 2 tablespoons of the chives and white pepper.

Melt the butter in a large nonstick skillet over medium heat. Add the shallots and sauté until tender and golden, stirring often, about 5 minutes. Add the egg mixture and cook until almost set, stirring occasionally, about 4 minutes. Stir in the salmon and cook about 1 minute longer, then add salt to taste. Garnish with the remaining 2 tablespoons of chives.

WHITE WINE POACHED EGGS

Serves 4

intro

Poaching eggs requires some type of acidity in the poaching liquid to make the eggs hold their shape. I like to poach eggs in white wine because it imparts a wonderfully rich, pungent and unexpected flavor. Look for the freshest eggs you can buy, as they hold their shape better than eggs with a little age on them. Poached eggs are just the thing to top a salad of baby greens and crisp bacon, a bed of golden brown breakfast potatoes, or an open-faced brunch sandwich made with toasted English muffins spread with a soft herb cheese and thin slices of smoked ham.

ingredients

8 fresh eggs
2 cups white wine
2 cups water

method

To poach the eggs, bring the wine and water to a vigorous boil in a large shallow pan. Break four eggs into four individual ramekins or small containers. Use a spoon to swirl the liquid in the pot in a clockwise direction, forming a current of sorts. Reduce the heat to a solid simmer and add the eggs, one at a time, into the places where the liquid is bubbling so the bubbles spin the eggs. Poach the eggs for 3 minutes, or until the yolks are set but still soft to the touch. Lift the eggs out of the pot with a slotted spoon and drain them on a clean kitchen towel or paper towels. Repeat with the remaining eggs.

CITRUS CHIVE HOLLANDAISE SAUCE

Makes about 2 cups

intro

Hollandaise turns a mere omelet, asparagus, or a grilled steak into heaven and this hollandaise is so simple to make using a blender. The trick is fresh citrus: lemon, orange, even grapefruit works, but please be aware that this preparation, made in a blender, does not cook the egg yolks completely. If you are wary of raw eggs, try using the store-bought pasteurized kind, which works just fine. This Hollandaise is so fresh and flavorful that it will become one of your "go to" final touches.

ingredients

8 egg yolks
1 tablespoon whipping cream
3 tablespoons fresh lemon, orange or grapefruit juice
Salt, freshly ground pepper and a dash of hot pepper sauce
4 sticks unsalted butter, hot
1/4 cup freshly chopped chives
Pepper, to taste

method

Place the egg yolks, cream, citrus juice and seasonings in a blender and blend until the mixture is frothy. With the blender running, SLOWLY pour the HOT melted butter into the egg mixture. The sauce will thicken as the butter blends with the egg yolks. Stir in the chives by hand and serve immediately or hold the sauce on a warm burner until ready to serve.

GARDEN FRITTATA

Serves 8

intro

A frittata—the Italian version of an omelet—is a gorgeous dish to set out for your guests. Frittatas make the perfect brunch centerpiece, cold dish for a picnic or a quick and clever "breakfast for dinner" meal. Frittatas have a texture firmer than omelets and no flipping is required! Served "unfolded" and cut into wedges, it's also easy to portion out servings. My favorite frittatas are made with a combination of flavors: mushrooms and asparagus, tomato and caramelized onion, smoked salmon and mascarpone, prosciutto and Parmesan or eggplant and goat cheese. This frittata is finished to a puffy golden brown under the broiler, so be sure your pan has an oven-proof handle.

ingredients

2 tablespoons unsalted butter
1 tablespoon extra-virgin olive oil
1 medium yellow onion, halved and sliced
8 shitake mushrooms, sliced
1/2 bunch asparagus, trimmed and cut into 1-inch pieces
8 large eggs
1/2 cup shredded Fontina cheese
2 ounces goat cheese, crumbled
1 tablespoon chopped fresh parsley
1 tablespoon chopped fresh chives
20 small cherry tomatoes, cut in half
Salt and pepper, to taste

method

Preheat the oven to 375°F. In a medium nonstick skillet with an oven-proof handle, heat the butter and oil over medium-low heat. Add the onions, season with salt and pepper and cook, stirring often, until caramelized, about 20 minutes. Increase the heat to medium-high and add the mushrooms. Sauté 2 minutes, then add the asparagus pieces and sauté 3 minutes more, stirring often. Add the tomatoes and stir to combine.

Beat the eggs lightly and stir in the cheeses and the herbs. Season with salt and pepper.

Add the egg mixture to the vegetables in the pan and lower the heat to medium low. Cook the frittata on top of the stove, pulling the eggs away from side of pan with a spatula, so that the uncooked portion runs to the sides. When the eggs start to set but the surface is still runny, place the frittata in the oven and bake until puffed and golden, about 8 minutes. Carefully slice the frittata into wedges and serve warm or at room temperature.

EGGNOG FRENCH TOAST

Serves 6

intro

Eggnog French Toast is the answer for holiday brunches for family and friends….Just assemble everything the night before, bake in the oven, and prepare yourself for the "how did you manage to find time to make a gourmet brunch?" compliments!   Add some real maple syrup to your shopping list for this dish, or dust with a snowfall of powdered sugar.

ingredients

4 cups homemade or store-bought eggnog
1 cup heavy cream
4 whole eggs
1 teaspoon ground nutmeg
1 teaspoon ground cinnamon
Twelve 2-inch thick slices Challah, egg bread or brioche
1 stick (8 tablespoons) unsalted butter, melted

method

Whisk the first 4 ingredients in a large baking dish or casserole. Place the bread slices in a single layer and turn to coat with the custard. Cover and refrigerate at least 6 hours or overnight. Remove the baking dish from the refrigerator and bring to room temperature.

Drizzle the French toast with half of the melted butter and bake for 10 minutes. Turn the bread slices over, drizzle them with the remaining butter and bake until golden brown and crisp on the outside but soft on the inside, about 6 minutes longer.

Serve dusted with powdered sugar and drizzled with maple syrup.

LEMON RICOTTA PANCAKES with BLUEBERRY MAPLE SYRUP

Makes 10 Pancakes

intro

This recipe makes fluffy, moist and fresh tasting pancakes. I love the zing from the lemon juice and the creaminess of the ricotta, topped with the sweetness of syrup. The fresh berry syrup is colorful and adds a concentrated flavor that you cannot find in bottled syrup. These pancakes are so delicious, your taste buds will go wild!

ingredients

1 cup ricotta cheese
2 eggs, lightly beaten
1 cup whole milk
1 cup all-purpose flour
1 tablespoon baking powder
1 tablespoon granulated sugar
Zest and juice of 1 lemon
Melted butter, for brushing the griddle
Toasted pecans, for garnish

For the Blueberry Syrup:
1 cup fresh blueberries
1 cup pure maple syrup
1 tablespoon fresh lemon juice

method

Combine the ricotta cheese, eggs and milk in a large mixing bowl and whisk to combine. Add the dry ingredients, the lemon zest and lemon juice and blend just until incorporated.

Heat a griddle or large sauté pan over medium high heat until it is hot enough to make drops of water scatter when sprinkled on the surface of the griddle. Brush the griddle with melted butter. Working in batches, pour a generous 1/4 cup of the batter onto the griddle to form each pancake. Once the pancake sets and you see small air bubbles form on the surface of the pancake, flip to cook the other side, brushing the griddle with additional melted butter, as necessary. Serve the pancakes topped with the Blueberry Maple Syrup and a sprinkling of toasted pecans.

For the Blueberry Syrup, combine the blueberries and maple syrup over medium heat in a small saucepan. Simmer the syrup until the blueberries burst, about 3 minutes. Strain the syrup through a fine mesh strainer, pressing on the solids. Discard the solids. Stir the lemon juice into the syrup and serve.

APPLE-GLAZED SAUSAGES

Serves 8

intro

Whether you are serving eggs, crispy waffles or French toast, these apple-glazed sausages are the ideal side dish. Southern food lovers might even serve these over grits! The apple juice, apple jelly and maple syrup create a delicious glaze that coats the sausages until they glisten with flavor. I recommend using smoked chicken sausage, turkey sausage, kielbasa or your favorite links.

ingredients

2 pounds cooked sausage of your choice, sliced
1/4 cup apple juice
1/4 cup apple jelly
1/4 cup maple syrup

method

Combine the sausage pieces and apple juice in a large sauté pan. Bring to a boil over medium heat, then cover and cook for 5 minutes. Remove the lid and reduce the heat to low. Continue cooking the sausage for 5 minutes more, turning the sausages frequently.

Add the apple jelly and maple syrup and cook over medium heat, turning to coat the sausages with the glaze.

Starters and Snacks

The Famous Hot Clam Dip

Chili Glazed Chicken Wings

Pistachio, Blue Cheese and Fig Puff Pastry Twists

Warm Blue Cheese Dip

Coconut Shrimp with
Apricot Ginger Dipping Sauce

Sweet and Sour Meatballs

Zucchini Caponata

Sweet and Spicy Cashews

Spicy Roasted Olives

Creamy Chipotle Hummus

THE FAMOUS HOT CLAM DIP

Serves 8

intro

Cut out the center of a round French bread and form chunks from the inside of the loaf. When ready to serve, pour the clam dip into the hollowed-out bread and serve with the bread chunks, for dipping. This is one of my favorite comforting buffet dishes, as the dip can be served either hot or cold.

ingredients

Two 8-ounce packages cream cheese, softened
2 tablespoons yellow onion, grated
2 tablespoons beer
2 teaspoons lemon juice
1 teaspoon Worcestershire sauce
1 teaspoon hot pepper sauce
Three 6.5 ounce cans minced clams, drained

method

Preheat the oven to 350°F. In a medium-size bowl combine the cream cheese, onion, beer, Worcestershire sauce, lemon juice and hot pepper sauce. Mix well, then fold the clams into the mixture. Pour the clam mixture into a shallow baking dish.

Bake for 20 minutes or until heated through and serve warm.

Serve with French bread cubes, chips or crackers.

CHILI GLAZED CHICKEN WINGS

Serves 6

intro

One of the ultimate finger foods, these chili glazed chicken wings practically jump off peoples plates! Easy to eat with one hand, your guests will be licking their fingers and filling their plates with these. Serve with shots of chilled sake.

ingredients

1/4 cup olive oil
3 tablespoons chopped cilantro
3 tablespoons soy sauce
2 tablespoons minced garlic
2 tablespoons grated ginger
1/2 teaspoon red pepper flakes
2 pounds chicken wings
1 cup rice wine vinegar
1/2 cup brown sugar
1/2 cup water
1 tablespoon store bought chili-garlic sauce
1/4 cup sliced scallions

method

Combine the olive oil, cilantro, soy sauce, garlic, ginger and red pepper flakes in a large mixing bowl. Add the wings and toss to coat well. Marinate in the refrigerator for at least 2 hours or overnight. To cook, drain the wings from the marinade and place on a baking sheet. Bake at 400°F for 20 minutes, or until the wings are cooked through and golden brown.

For the sauce, combine the rice wine vinegar, brown sugar, water and chili-garlic sauce in a sauce pot. Bring the mixture to a boil, reduce the heat and simmer for 20 minutes or until thickened. Pour the glaze over the cooked wings and toss to coat. Garnish with the chopped scallions.

PISTACHIO, BLUE CHEESE and FIG PUFF PASTRY TWISTS

Makes 16 Twists

intro

These easy to make pastry twists require simply rolling out store bought puff pastry, topping and twisting. Simple and sensational!

ingredients

1 package frozen puff pastry, thawed
1 egg
1 tablespoon cold water
3/4 cup fig preserves
3/4 cup crumbled blue cheese
1 1/4 cups pistachios, toasted

method

Preheat the oven to 400ºF.

Unfold the puff pastry sheets onto a lightly floured work surface. Roll out both sheets just enough to smooth out the creases (the pastry sheets will only increase in size about an inch on all sides after rolling out). Beat the egg and water and set the egg wash aside.

Spread the fig preserve evenly over one pastry sheet. Sprinkle the blue cheese and 3/4 cup pistachios over the preserves. Lay the second pastry sheet over the top.

Brush the top of the pastry with the beaten egg. Sprinkle 1/4 cup chopped pistachios over the egg wash, lightly pressing the nuts into the pastry. Turn the pastry over and repeat with the egg wash and remaining pistachios.

Cut the pastry across the shortest width into 1/2-inch strips. Twist each strip and lay 1/2-inch apart on a silicone baking mat or parchment paper-lined baking sheet. Bake for 15 minutes or until puffed and golden.

WARM BLUE CHEESE DIP

Makes about 5 Cups

intro

Tell your guests you'll be serving a warm blue cheese dip and they'll flock to your party! Serve this dip with pieces of crusty French or sourdough bread, slices of green apple or pear, sweet potato fries, or let guests drizzle warm blue cheese dip over seared, rare beef slices. Pair this dip with a tart cocktail.

ingredients

4 cups heavy cream
12 ounces Cambozola cheese, crumbled (or other creamy blue cheese)
Freshly ground black pepper
3 tablespoons freshly chopped parsley

method

Place the cream in a saucepot and bring to a simmer over medium heat. Simmer until the cream is reduced by one-third. Over low heat, slowly add the cheese and whisk until the cheese is melted and the mixture is smooth. Add the pepper and parsley and serve warm.

COCONUT SHRIMP with APRICOT GINGER DIPPING SAUCE

Serves 6 as an Appetizer

intro

A buffet with shrimp equals happy people standing next to the table. Next thing you know they'll be eating, talking…and it's a party! Crisp and easy to handle, these offer a snappy blend of sweet and spicy flavors. Serve them with a crisp sparkling wine, a fruity Riesling or a Sauvignon Blanc.

ingredients

1/3 cup curry powder
3/4 cup all-purpose flour
1 3/4 teaspoons salt
3 large eggs
1/3 cup heavy cream
1 1/4 cups shredded coconut
1 1/2 cups Panko crumbs (Japanese bread crumbs)
1/4 teaspoon cayenne pepper
1 teaspoon dried dill
1 pound large shrimp (14 to 18 per pound), shelled and deveined
Canola or Grapeseed oil, for deep-frying

APRICOT GINGER DIPPING SAUCE
1 cup apricot jam
2 tablespoons freshly grated ginger
2 tablespoons Dijon mustard
2 tablespoons freshly squeezed lime juice

method

To make the Apricot Ginger Dipping Sauce, combine the sauce ingredients in a blender or food processor and blend until smooth.

In a shallow bowl, mix the curry powder, flour and salt together. In another bowl, whisk the eggs and cream together. In a third bowl, combine the coconut, bread crumbs, cayenne and dill.

Dredge 4 shrimp in the flour mixture, then dip them in the egg mixture and coat them in the coconut mixture. Dip each shrimp again, into the egg mixture, then coat one more time in the coconut mixture. In a heavy skillet or deep fryer, heat 1 to 2 inches of oil to 375°F. Deep-fry the shrimp in batches until golden brown, about 3 minutes. Using a slotted spoon, transfer to paper towels to drain. Serve hot with the dipping sauce.

SWEET and SOUR MEATBALLS

Serves 8 as an Appetizer

intro

Meatballs are always charming and satisfying. These Sweet and Sour Meatballs are delicious on their own—served on party skewers—or as Italian "sliders" on a slice of toasted garlic bread, topped with a shaving of good Parmesan. A Zinfandel is the perfect pairing.

ingredients

Two 28-ounce cans Italian-style tomatoes
One 14 1/2 ounce can beef broth
1 1/2 cups finely chopped onion
1/2 cup golden brown sugar
4 large garlic cloves, minced
1 tablespoon fresh lemon juice
2 pounds lean ground beef
1 cup toasted breadcrumbs
2 teaspoons salt
1 teaspoon ground pepper
1/2 teaspoon ground allspice
2 large eggs, beaten to blend

method

Pour the tomatoes with their juices into a large pot. Using a potato masher crush the tomatoes into large chunks. Add the broth, 1/2 cup onion, brown sugar, half of the garlic and 1 tablespoon of lemon juice. Place the pot over medium heat and bring to a boil. Reduce the heat to low and simmer the sauce while preparing the meatballs.

Combine the ground beef, breadcrumbs, salt, pepper, allspice, remaining 1 cup onion and remaining garlic in a large mixing bowl. Add the eggs and blend well. Shape the mixture into 1 to 1 1/2-inch balls. Gently drop the meatballs into the simmering sauce. Partially cover the pot and simmer over very low heat until the meatballs are cooked through and tender and the sauce is thick, about 30 minutes. Spoon off any fat from the top of the sauce and serve.

chef's tip

These meatballs can be made 2 days ahead. After cooking, allow the meatballs to cool completely, then cover and chill. Warm the meatballs over low heat before serving.

ZUCCHINI CAPONATA

Yields about 5 cups

intro

While this Italian vegetable dish is usually made with eggplant, we find it's every bit as delicious when made with zucchini. Caponata is a dip or spread, served cold or warm. It's a wonderful topping for bruschetta or crostini (thin pieces of an Italian loaf, such as ciabatta or French baguette, slow-toasted till crisp)...or pile it on toasted pita chips for a true Mediterranean treat.

ingredients

1/4 cup extra virgin olive oil
4 cups zucchini, cut into 1-inch chunks
1 yellow onion, diced
4 garlic cloves, peeled and minced
2 large or 4 small tomatoes, seeded and diced
1 tablespoon granulated sugar
Salt and pepper
1 cup cherry tomatoes, halved
3 tablespoons capers, drained
1/2 cup black or green olives, pitted and halved

method

Heat the oil over medium heat in a large sauté pan. Add the zucchini, onion, garlic and tomatoes and cook, covered, for 10 minutes, stirring once halfway through cooking (the vegetables should become tender, but won't brown very much). Remove the lid and cook for an additional 15 to 20 minutes, stirring often, until most of the liquid has evaporated and the vegetables begin to caramelize slightly. Season the mixture with salt and pepper and stir in the sugar. Continue cooking the caponata about 5 minutes longer, until the vegetables are dry and golden. Remove the pan from the heat and stir in the cherry tomatoes, capers and olives. Serve warm or refrigerate until ready to serve.

SWEET and SPICY CASHEWS

Serves 6

intro

My sweet and spicy cashews are a tasty finger food for a party! The salty and sweet combination is an ideal counterpoint to cocktails.

ingredients

1 pound cashew nuts
2 tablespoons coarsely chopped fresh rosemary leaves
1/2 teaspoon cayenne
2 teaspoons dark brown sugar
2 teaspoons kosher salt
1 tablespoon melted butter

method

Preheat the oven to 375°F.

Place the nuts on an ungreased baking sheet and bake for about ten minutes until they are warmed through. Combine the rosemary, pepper, sugar, salt and butter in a large bowl. Toss the warm nuts with the rosemary mixture until the nuts are completely coated. Serve warm.

SPICY ROASTED OLIVES

Serves 6 to 8

intro

These roasted olives combine the best of salty, savory, spicy and tangy. Serve them with a sharp cheese, slices of prosciutto and a bottle of chilled Pinot Grigio.

ingredients

3 cups mixed green and black olives with pits
4 sprigs fresh rosemary
1 fresh red chili, sliced thinly
4 whole garlic cloves, peeled
2 tangerines or small oranges, rind left on and sliced
1/2 cup extra-virgin olive oil
1 tablespoon red wine vinegar

method

Preheat the oven to 300°F. In a small roasting pan combine the olives, rosemary, chili, garlic cloves, tangerine slices, olive oil and vinegar and toss to combine. Cover the pan with foil and bake for 1 hour.

Serve warm or at room temperature.

CREAMY CHIPOTLE HUMMUS

Serves 8

intro

I love this smoky delicious dip, full of garlic and heat from the chipotles. Chipotles are dried smoked jalapeños that come packed in a can of adobo sauce. Tahini, the sesame seed paste that gives hummus its distinctive flavor, along with the chipotles in adobo sauce can be found in the ethnic section of your local grocery store. Try serving your homemade hummus with toasted pita chips or bagel chips and an assortment of crunchy vegetables, such as baby carrots, cucumber, zucchini slices or snow peas.

ingredients

Two 15 ounce cans garbanzo beans
1/2 cup reserved liquid from a can of garbanzo beans
1/4 cup tahini
4 tablespoons fresh lemon juice
3 tablespoons extra virgin olive oil
2 teaspoons adobo sauce from a can of chipotle chilies (or to taste)
1 large garlic clove, minced
1 teaspoon ground cumin
Salt and white pepper
1/2 cup toasted pine nuts

method

Drain the garbanzo beans, reserving 1/2 cup of the liquid from the cans. In a food processor combine the drained garbanzo beans, the 1/2 cup of reserved liquid, tahini, lemon juice, olive oil, adobo sauce, garlic and cumin. Puree the mixture until smooth then season with salt and pepper. (The hummus can be made a day ahead, covered and refrigerated until ready to serve. Bring the hummus to room temperature before serving.)

To serve, transfer the hummus to a serving bowl and make a small well in the center of the hummus using the back of a teaspoon. Fill the well with a tablespoon of olive oil and garnish the hummus with the toasted pine nuts and freshly chopped parsley.

Savory and Sweet Fondues

Garlic Two Cheese Fondue

Classic Cheese Fondue

Italian Cheese Fondue

Apple Cider Cheddar Fondue

Fudge Fondue

Peanut Butter and Chocolate Fondue

Caramel Fondue

GARLIC TWO CHEESE FONDUE

Serves 6

intro

This fondue is a heartier version of the classic, perfect for dipping cooked sausage, potatoes and ham. Balance the strong, savory flavors of this fondue with icy cold ale and a light, palate cleansing fruit sorbet for dessert.

ingredients

8 ounces Monterey jack cheese, coarsely grated
8 ounces Fontina cheese, coarsely grated
2 tablespoons cornstarch
2 cups dry white wine
2 teaspoons minced garlic
Salt and freshly ground black pepper
1/4 teaspoon freshly grated nutmeg

For Dipping:
Cooked baby potatoes, halved
Cooked sliced sausage
Cooked, cubed ham
Blanches Asparagus and broccoli
Bread Cubes

method

In a large mixing bowl, combine the two cheeses with the flour and toss to coat well. In a fondue pot or saucepot, bring the wine and garlic to a simmer over medium-low heat. Add half of the cheese and whisk until melted. Add the remaining cheese and whisk until completely melted and combined. Season with salt, pepper and nutmeg, and simmer until the mixture is smooth, about 2 minutes more.

Serve with potatoes, sausage, vegetables and bread, for dipping.

CLASSIC CHEESE FONDUE

Serves 6

intro

Fondue brings everyone to the table and keeps them together, dipping, eating and talking. This classic fondue is a cheesy melt of aromatic cheeses, white wine and Kirsch, a cherry brandy. Fondue is deceivingly rich…so crusty breads, apples, grapes, pears and blanched vegetables such as asparagus or broccoli provide a great mix of textures for delicious dipping!

ingredients

8 ounces Emmentaler cheese, coarsely grated
8 ounces Gruyere cheese, coarsely grated
2 tablespoons cornstarch
1 garlic clove
2 cups dry white wine
1 tablespoon lemon juice
3 tablespoons Kirsch
1/8 teaspoon ground nutmeg

For Dipping:
Bread cubes, apples wedges, blanched vegetables

method

In a large mixing bowl, combine the two cheeses with the flour and toss to coat well. Rub a fondue pot or saucepot with the garlic clove to extract the flavor, then discard the garlic clove. Pour the wine into the pot and bring to a simmer over low heat. Add the cheese and whisk until melted. Add the lemon juice, Kirsch and nutmeg and stir to combine. Reduce the heat to low and serve the fondue with the classic accompaniments.

ITALIAN CHEESE FONDUE

Serves 6

intro

Fondue might be a Swiss dish, but with a few different cheeses and dippers, it's an Italian feast! Italian cheeses and meats make the perfect dip for foccacia bread, breadsticks and apple slices. I've even dipped a few items from the classic antipasto plate, such as olives, hard salami and sun dried tomatoes. If you can't get prosciutto, substitute a good quality, smoked bacon or pancetta. A robust red zinfandel or Prosecco—the Italian sparkling wine—are a great match.

ingredients

8 ounces Fontina cheese, coarsely grated
8 ounces grated Provolone cheese, coarsely grated
2 tablespoons cornstarch
6 ounces prosciutto, thinly sliced and chopped
2 cups dry white wine
2 tablespoons chopped chives
Salt and freshly ground pepper

For Dipping:
Italian breadsticks, strips of focaccia bread, apples slices

method

In a large mixing bowl, combine the two cheeses with the flour and toss to coat well. Sauté the pancetta in a fondue pot or saucepot over medium heat until crisp and golden, about 10 minutes. Transfer the pancetta to a plate and pour off any excess oil from the pot.

Pour the wine into the same saucepot and bring it to a boil. Reduce the heat to a simmer and slowly whisk in the cornstarch-coated cheeses, blending well after each addition to ensure that the cheese is melted. Stir in the cooked prosciutto and the chives. Season the fondue with salt and pepper. Serve the Italian Fondue with breadsticks, bread and apple slices for dipping.

APPLE CIDER CHEDDAR FONDUE

Serves 6

intro

This fondue is a bit like the comfort food favorite of a slice of apple pie with sharp cheddar cheese…The flavors were just meant for each other! The aroma of apple cider simmering with cheese is too good to resist. Dip into this fondue with slices of roasted or grilled chicken, pieces of smoked ham, apple or pear slices, tender dried apricots and purple grapes.

ingredients

16 ounces sharp Cheddar cheese, shredded
2 tablespoons cornstarch
2 cups apple cider
Salt and freshly ground pepper
1/8 teaspoon ground nutmeg

For Dipping:
Cooked meats, Bread cubes, apples wedges

method

In a large mixing bowl, combine the two cheeses with the flour and toss to coat well. In a fondue pot or saucepot, bring the apple cider to a simmer over medium-low heat. Add half of the cheese and whisk until melted. Add the remaining cheese and whisk until completely melted and combined. Season with salt, pepper and nutmeg, and simmer until the mixture is smooth, about 2 minutes more.

Serve with meats, bread and apple wedges for dipping.

FUDGE FONDUE

Serves 8

intro

This fondue is chocolate heaven! It's perfect for dipping fruit (I especially like tangerine segments and blueberries), cubes of cake, brownies or cookies. A chocolate fondue is the ultimate "girls' night in" treat, as well as a perfect birthday delight.

ingredients

1 pound bittersweet chocolate, chopped
1 cup sweetened condensed milk
1 cup whole milk

For Dipping:
Cubes of Pound Cake, Pretzels, Marshmallows, Strawberries,
Bananas, etc.

method

Combine the two milks in a saucepot and bring the mixture to a boil over medium heat. Add the chopped chocolate and remove the pan from the heat. Let the mixture sit for two minutes, to allow the chocolate to melt, then stir using a rubber spatula until the mixture is satiny and fully blended.

chef's tip

To flavor the Fudge Fondue, infuse the milk with your favorite spice, such as cinnamon or vanilla.

PEANUT BUTTER and CHOCOLATE FONDUE

Serves 6

intro

This fondue is like a candy bar—rich chocolate and peanut butter, all in one bite—and the condensed milk makes the fondue extra sweet and creamy. Tend to the pot while the ingredients are melting together, as the high sugar content might scorch. I can't think of anything better than dipping into this fondue with a piece of brownie or peanut butter cookie, followed by a cold glass of milk.

ingredients

1 pound (16 ounces) dark or milk chocolate, chopped
1/2 cup creamy peanut butter
1/2 cup sweetened condensed milk

For Dipping:
Cubes of pound cake, pretzels, marshmallows, strawberries, sliced bananas

method

Combine the chocolate, peanut butter and sweetened condensed milk in a fondue pot or saucepot and bring the mixture to a simmer over medium-low heat, stirring constantly to combine and avoid scorching. Once the chocolate is melted, stir the mixture until the fondue is satiny and fully blended.

Serve with sweets for dipping.

CARAMEL FONDUE

Serves 8

intro

This rich caramel flavor compliments fruit perfectly, but it also works for cake and cookies. Crunchy almond biscotti, for dipping, and steaming hot cappuccino, for sipping, would make this an elegant finish to dinner.

ingredients

2 1/2 cups heavy whipping cream
1 cup granulated sugar
4 tablespoons water
2 tablespoons of your favorite liqueur, Cognac, Amaretto
    or Grand Marnier (optional)
1 tablespoon cold unsalted butter
Pinch of salt

For Dipping:
Sliced pears and/or apples, strawberries, sliced bananas, cookies, cubes of
    pound cake

method

Place the cream in a small saucepot and bring to a simmer over medium heat. Keep warm.

Combine the sugar and water in a fondue pot or heavy-bottomed saucepot. Stir constantly over low heat until the sugar dissolves. Increase the heat to medium-high and boil without stirring until the mixture is a deep amber color, occasionally swirling the pan to keep the sugar from crystallizing on the sides of the pot. A deep caramel color should develop after about 3 minutes of cooking.

Once the sugar is deep caramel in color, remove the pot from the heat and carefully add the warm cream to the caramel. Replace the pot over medium heat and simmer until the caramel sauce is smooth and slightly reduced, about 5 minutes. Add your liqueur of choice and cook 1 minute longer. Remove the caramel from the heat and whisk in the butter and salt.

Serve the fondue with apples, pears, strawberries, bananas, cake, cookies, etc.

Sensational Soups

Oriental Chicken Soup

Corn and Crab Chowder

Creamy Vegetable Chowder

French Onion Soup

Classic Minestrone Soup

Roasted Butternut Squash Soup

Spicy Split Pea Soup

ORIENTAL CHICKEN SOUP

Serves 6

intro

This delicious soup will cure a cold and hold back the cold weather chill, too. Instead of chicken, add additional vegetables and a delicious vegetarian broth is created. Add the easy-to-make dumplings and you have a hearty meal. Freshly chopped cilantro or parsley and crispy snow peas add the final touch before serving. You'll want to use your biggest soup pot and make extra, because everyone will come back for more!

ingredients

For the Broth:
1 whole chicken
1 onion, cut in half
3 carrots, peeled and halved
1/4 cup fresh ginger, peeled and cut into pieces
8 garlic cloves
1 handful (combined) of fresh thyme, parsley and dill
2 bay leaves
10 black peppercorns
Salt, to taste

For the Garnish:
12 snow peas
1 carrot, cut into match sticks
Chopped cilantro
Chopped scallions

For The Dumplings:
2 cooked chicken breasts
1 tablespoon fresh ginger, grated
2 scallions, chopped
1 small carrot, minced
2 tablespoons cilantro, chopped
2 tablespoons soy sauce
24 small wonton wrappers

method

In a large stockpot, place all of the ingredients and cover with water. Bring to a simmer over medium heat and cook for 1 1/2 to 2 hours. Remove the chicken from the pot and strain the broth.

continued on next page

ORIENTAL CHICKEN SOUP

Continued

To make the dumplings, combine all of the ingredients in a food processor and pulse to chop finely. Spoon 1 tablespoon of the filling into the center of each wonton wrapper. Moisten one side of the wrapper with a bit of water and fold the other side over, pressing to seal, creating a half moon shape.

To serve, drop the dumplings, snow peas and matchstick carrots into the simmering broth and cook for one minute. Ladle the soup into bowls and garnish with chopped cilantro and scallions.

CORN and CRAB CHOWDER

Serves 6

intro

As a seafood lover, I dream of chowders filled with sweet tidbits from the catch of the day, simmered with the perfect blend of veggies in a rich, creamy broth. This soup tastes like your favorites from the wharf. You can easily prepare this chowder with your family's preferred seafood-lobster, clams, salmon, shrimp-just make sure it is the freshest you can find. Don't forget lots of good sourdough or French bread for dipping.

ingredients

1 tablespoon extra-virgin olive oil
2 tablespoons unsalted butter
1 medium yellow onion, diced
3 celery stalks, diced
1 small red bell pepper, seeded and diced
1 Yukon gold potato, peeled and diced
1 medium red potato, peeled and diced
Salt and freshly ground pepper, to taste
1 bay leaf
1 tablespoon Old Bay Seasoning
3 tablespoons all-purpose flour
2 cups chicken broth
1 1/2 cups half and half
1 1/2 cups whole milk
2 cups corn kernels
8 ounces jumbo lump crab meat

For Garnish:
1 cup Pepper Jack cheese, shredded
6 strips bacon, cooked till crisp and crumbled
1/2 cup green onion, thinly sliced

method

Heat the oil and butter in a large soup pot. Add the onion and celery and season with salt and pepper. Sauté until tender, about 10 minutes. Add the red pepper and potatoes, add the bay leaf, season with the Old Bay and sauté 5 minutes more.

continued on next page

CORN and CRAB CHOWDER

Continued

Sprinkle the flour over the vegetables and cook 2 minutes, stirring constantly. Add the broth, milk and half and half and adjust the seasoning.

Bring the soup just to a simmer and cook 10 minutes. Add the corn and crab and simmer 15 minutes more. Remove the bay leaf, adjust the seasoning and test the potatoes for tenderness. (Simmer longer if necessary.)

To serve, ladle the soup into bread bowls or soup bowls and garnish with shredded cheese, crumbled bacon and green onions.

CREAMY VEGETABLE CHOWDER

Serves 6

intro

There's something very reassuring about a mellow soup of winter vegetables when it's cold outside. The potato, squash and root vegetables combined with sweet and earthy spices is a perfect first course, or a hearty main course. This soup is easy to prepare ahead of time and elegant enough for holiday entertaining.

ingredients

6 tablespoons unsalted butter
1 tablespoon minced garlic
2 medium onions, coarsely chopped
1 turnip, peeled and chopped
1 carrot, peeled and chopped
1 medium white potato, peeled and chopped
3/4 pound winter squash, preferably butternut or pumpkin, peeled and diced or One 15 oz. can cooked pumpkin
1/4 teaspoon ground cumin
1/2 teaspoon nutmeg
1/2 teaspoon ground coriander
1 teaspoon ground ginger
2 cups chicken broth
2 bay leaves
1 cup Half and Half
Salt and freshly ground pepper
Croutons, for garnish
Fried Sage Leaves, for garnish

method

Melt the butter in a large, heavy pot. Over medium heat, add the garlic, onion and all of the vegetables and sauté gently, without browning, for 10 to 15 minutes, stirring occasionally to prevent sticking. When the vegetables begin to soften add the spices and sauté two minutes more. Add chicken broth and bay leaves, cover, and simmer for 45 minutes or until all vegetables are completely soft. Discard bay leaves. Puree in a food processor or blender in 2 cup portions. Reheat gently, add the Half and Half and season to taste. Garnish with croutons and fried sage leaves.

FRENCH ONION SOUP

Serves 6

intro

This classic soup gets its incredible flavor from slow-cooked, well-caramelized onions. You can roast the onions in the oven or caramelize them on top of the stove, just take your time to bring out all the natural sugar and flavor in the onions. Use Maui or Sweet Vidalia onions in place of the basic yellow onion, for extra sweetness.

ingredients

1/2 stick unsalted butter (for stove-top cooking only)
2 tablespoons extra-virgin olive oil
8 cups yellow onions (about 2 pounds), thinly sliced
Salt and pepper, to taste
8 cups beef broth
1/2 cup Cognac, or other good Brandy
Eight 1/2-inch thick slices of French bread, toasted
3/4 pound Gruyere cheese, coarsely grated

method

TO ROAST THE ONIONS IN THE OVEN:
Preheat oven to 450°. Toss the sliced onions with the olive oil and place in a roasting pan (do not use the butter if you are roasting the onions). Season with salt and pepper. Roast the onions, stirring every 10 minutes, for about 25-30 minutes or until the onions are golden. Remove the pan from the oven and add the cognac, scraping the bottom to loosen and dissolve any caramelized bits. Transfer the onion mixture to a soup pot and add the beef broth. Bring to a simmer and allow the soup to cook slowly for 45 minutes. (Finish Soup by following Serving Directions on next page.)

TO CARAMELIZE THE ONIONS ON TOP OF THE STOVE:
Heat the butter and oil in a heavy saucepan over moderate heat. Add the onions and season with salt and pepper. Cook slowly until tender and caramelized, stirring frequently, until they are a deep caramel color, about 25 to 30 minutes. Add the cognac and deglaze, scraping up any browned bits from the bottom of the pan. Add the beef broth, bring to a simmer and allow the soup to cook slowly for 45 minutes.

To Serve: Divide the soup among 4 ovenproof bowls. Arrange the toasted bread on top of the soup and sprinkle generously with the grated cheese. Arrange the bowls on a cookie sheet and place under a preheated broiler until the cheese melts and forms a crust over the tops of the bowls. Serve immediately.

CLASSIC MINESTRONE

Serves 6

intro

Every great buffet should offer some vegetarian options, and hearty minestrone is one of the best. To convert the dish into a hearty ribollita (ribollita means "reboiled' and refers to a Tuscan bread-based soup), ladle the soup over a few slices of hearty bread in a soup bowl. Drizzle with a little olive oil and allow the bread to soak up the flavors. Pair the meal with a zesty red, such as a Chianti or Rioja.

ingredients

2 tablespoons extra-virgin olive oil
1 yellow onion, diced
2 carrots, peeled and diced
2 celery stalks, diced
3 ounces thinly sliced pancetta, coarsely chopped
2 garlic cloves, minced
1 pound Swiss chard, stems trimmed, leaves coarsely chopped
1 russet potato, peeled, cubed

One 14 1/2-ounce can diced tomatoes
1 fresh rosemary sprig
One 15-ounce can cannellini beans, drained, rinsed
4 cups chicken broth
1 ounce piece Parmesan cheese rind
2 tablespoons chopped fresh Italian parsley leaves
Salt and freshly ground pepper
Pesto (recipe follows)

method

Heat the oil in a heavy large pot over medium heat. Add the onion, carrots, celery, pancetta, and garlic. Sauté until the onion is translucent, about 10 minutes. Add the Swiss chard and potato; sauté for 2 minutes. Add the tomatoes and rosemary sprig. Simmer until the chard is wilted and the tomatoes break down, about 10 minutes.

continued on next page

CLASSIC MINESTRONE

continued

Meanwhile, blend 3/4 cup of the beans with 1/4 cup of the broth in a processor until almost smooth. Add the pureed bean mixture, remaining broth, and Parmesan cheese rind to the vegetable mixture. Simmer until the potato pieces are tender, stirring occasionally, about 15 minutes. Stir in the whole beans and parsley. Simmer until the beans are heated through and the soup is thick, about 5 minutes. Season with salt and pepper. Discard Parmesan rind and rosemary sprig.   Garnish each bowl with a spoonful of pesto and a sprinkling of Parmesan Cheese.

for the pesto

ingredients

- **3 large garlic cloves**
- **1/2 cup pine nuts**
- **2/3 cup grated Parmesan cheese**
- **Salt and freshly ground pepper**
- **3 cups loosely packed fresh basil leaves**
- **2/3 cup extra-virgin olive oil**

method

With the food processor running, drop in garlic and finely chop. Add the pine nuts, cheese, salt, pepper, and basil, and process until finely chopped. Add oil, blending until incorporated.

ROASTED BUTTERNUT SQUASH SOUP

Serves 6

intro

The creamy texture and heartiness of butternut squash are the essence of fall in a bowl. This beautiful soup gets added sweetness from the flavors of apple and leek. Roasted butternut squash soup is made for toppings, so be sure to offer guests a variety-such as chutney, roasted pumpkin seeds, crème fraiche, or pomegranate seeds.

ingredients

One 2-pound butternut squash, halved lengthwise and seeded
3 tablespoons extra-virgin olive oil
1 medium yellow onion, diced
1 large leek, white and pale green parts only, washed and chopped finely
1 large garlic clove, minced
1 Granny Smith apple, peeled and chopped
1/2 teaspoon ground nutmeg
4 cups low-salt chicken broth
4 ounces cream cheese
salt and pepper, to taste
Sour cream, apple slices and fried leeks, for garnish

method

Preheat the oven to 375°F. Spray a large glass baking dish with non-stick cooking spray. Place the squash cut side down in the prepared dish. Pierce each squash half several times with a sharp knife. Bake until the squash is tender, about 45 minutes. Using a large spoon, scrape the flesh into a mixing bowl and discard the peel.

In a soup pot, heat the olive oil. Add the onion and leek and sauté over medium heat until tender. Add the garlic, diced apple and nutmeg and sauté 2 minutes more. Add the roasted squash and broth and stir to combine. Simmer the mixture for 20 minutes to meld the flavors, then discard bay leaf. In a blender, purée the mixture in batches, adding in the cream cheese to blend thoroughly. Adjust the seasoning with salt and pepper to taste.

Serve the soup hot or cold, topped with sour cream, a thin apple slice and crispy fried leeks.

SPICY SPLIT PEA SOUP

Serves 6

intro

Dried split peas turn into something wonderful after a few hours in a pot. Creamy and satisfying, this soup is easy to prepare on top of the stove and even simpler when made in your slow cooker or crock pot. This recipe makes a fabulous, spicy version when chorizo is added. If you're not a chorizo lover, use a smoky ham hock to impart flavor, then remove the hock before pureeing the soup. The meat from the ham hock should fall off the bone, and you can add it back to the pureed soup when ready to serve.

ingredients

1 pound green split peas
10 cups chicken broth
1/2 pound diced chorizo (or a small ham hock)
1 yellow onion, cut in quarters and peeled
1 cup diced carrot
1/2 cup diced celery
1 clove garlic
2 bay leaves
Salt and freshly ground pepper

method

Combine all of the ingredients in a large soup pot. Cover the pot and bring the soup to a boil, then reduce the heat to simmer and cook the soup until the peas are tender about 1 hour. Remove the pot from the heat and remove the bay leaves. Using a hand-held immersion blender, or in batches in your food processor, puree the soup until smooth. Adjust the seasoning and serve.

chef's tip

This soup tastes better the next day, and the day after that, and…

Chicken and Turkey Every Way

Roast Chicken with Lemon, Honey and Thyme

Maple Glazed Chicken Wings

Pesto and Cheese Filled Chicken Breasts

Sauteed Chicken Breasts with Riesling
and Wild Mushrooms

Spanish Chicken with Rice

Raspberry Marinated Baked Chicken

Chicken Bruschetta

Lana's Chicken Cacciatore

Asian Turkey Burgers

Turkey Pot Pie

ROAST CHICKEN with LEMON, HONEY and THYME

Serves 8

intro

This chicken turns out moist and delicious every time! Filling the cavities of the chickens with the lemon rinds keeps the chicken juicy all the way through the cooking process…and the honey glaze makes for very satisfying comfort food. This crowd pleasing dish is my favorite simple Sunday Night Buffet.

ingredients

Two 3 1/2-pound chickens, giblets removed
Salt and freshly ground pepper
1 bunch fresh thyme
1 cup honey
6 tablespoons unsalted butter, at room temperature
3 lemons - zested, halved and juiced
12 cloves garlic, peeled

method

Preheat the oven to 400°F. Rinse the chickens under cold water, then pat dry with paper towels. Generously season the chickens, inside and out, with salt and pepper.

Remove the leaves from 8 sprigs of thyme. In a medium bowl, mix together the honey, butter, thyme leaves, lemon juice and lemon zest. Set aside.

Combine the lemon halves, remaining thyme sprigs and garlic and split the mixture to fill both chicken's cavities. Place the chickens in a large roasting pan and use a pastry brush to coat the outside of the chickens with the honey glaze. Roast the chickens in the center of the oven, basting every 15 minutes with the remaining glaze. Roast until a thermometer inserted into the deepest part of the thigh registers 165°F and juices run clear when the chicken is pierced with a knife, about 1 1/2 hours.

Remove the chickens from the oven and allow them to rest for 10 minutes before carving.

MAPLE GLAZED CHICKEN WINGS

Serves 6

intro

These are the ultimate finger-licking, delicious wings. They taste even better after marinating in the fridge overnight, but can easily be tossed with the sauce and baked right away for fabulous flavor. The generous amount of maple syrup and teriyaki sauce makes the wings caramelize to a rich brown color. Maple glazed chicken wings are poured into a casserole dish and baked with the marinade, making this an easy, no stress dish. Serve with a frosty beer, some extra napkins, and enjoy!

ingredients

4 pounds chicken wings
1 1/2 cups maple syrup
1/4 cup low sodium soy sauce
1/4 cup teriyaki sauce
1 tablespoon Dijon mustard
1/2 teaspoon cayenne pepper
4 garlic cloves, minced
Freshly ground pepper

method

Preheat the oven to 350°F.

Cut off the wing tips from the chicken wings and rinse the chicken wings thoroughly, then pat dry.

In a large mixing bowl combine the maple syrup, soy sauce, teriyaki sauce, mustard, garlic, cayenne and black pepper and whisk to combine. Add the chicken wings and toss to coat.

Line a large casserole dish with aluminum foil and pour the chicken wings with the marinade into the pan. Bake the wings for 45 minutes, tossing the wings twice during cooking. As the wings cook, the sauce will reduce and thicken. After 1 hour of cooking, increase the oven temperature to 425°F and cook an additional 45 minutes, tossing often.

PESTO and CHEESE FILLED CHICKEN BREASTS

Serves 4

intro

Lana had this signature recipe of hers published in Bon Appetit Magazine (so now you know where I acquired my passion for cooking….from my Mom!). Her garden-fresh Thyme Pesto is the star of this elegant entrée, but you can also use store bought or homemade basil pesto. Serve the chicken with Caramelized Shallots, Parsnips and Potatoes and a buttery, oaky Chardonnay (Lana's favorite!).

ingredients

THYME PESTO:
1 1/2 cups loosely packed fresh parsley
1/2 cup loosely packed fresh thyme leaves or 1 tablespoon dried, crumbled,
  plus 1/2 cup fresh parsley
1/2 cup (about 2 ounces) grated Parmesan cheese
1/2 cup toasted pine nuts or walnuts
2 garlic cloves
1/2 cup extra-virgin olive oil

For the CHICKEN:
4 boneless, skinless chicken breasts
4 ounces goat cheese
1/3 cup Thyme Pesto (recipe follows)
1 teaspoon minced shallot or green onion
2 tablespoons extra-virgin olive oil
All-purpose flour

method

Finely chop the first 5 ingredients in a food processor. With the machine running, gradually add the 1/2 cup olive oil. Continue processing until pesto is almost smooth. Season to taste with salt and pepper. (Pesto can be prepared up to 1 week ahead. Cover tightly and refrigerate.)

Preheat the oven to 350°F. Pound the chicken breasts between sheets of waxed paper to a thickness of 1/4-inch. Combine the goat cheese, pesto and shallot in a small bowl and mix well. Spread the underside of each chicken breast with 2 tablespoons of the cheese mixture. Starting at the long side of each chicken breast, roll up tightly, jelly roll style. Repeat with remaining chicken and cheese mixture.

Heat the olive oil in a large oven-proof skillet over medium-high heat. Season the chicken breasts with salt and pepper. Dredge each breast in flour and shake off any excess. Pan sauté the chicken breasts until golden brown on all sides, turning occasionally, about 4 minutes. Place the skillet in the oven and bake until the chicken is tender and cooked through, about 10 minutes.

SAUTEED CHICKEN BREASTS with RIESLING and WILD MUSHROOMS

Serves 6

intro

This is a simple, yet elegant dish you'll want to serve again and again. The creamy wine sauce is filled with earthy mushrooms and a hint of wine. What's not to love? I serve this dish with wild rice and a salad of micro greens with lemon vinaigrette. A classic, beautiful dinner your guests will remember.

ingredients

For the Chicken:
2 tablespoons unsalted butter
2 tablespoons extra virgin olive oil
6 boneless, skinless chicken breasts
2 teaspoons fresh thyme leaves
Salt and freshly ground pepper
1 cup all-purpose flour

For the Sauce:
1 tablespoon unsalted butter
1 cup sliced crimini mushrooms
1/2 cup sliced Shiitake mushrooms
1/4 cup Riesling
1/4 cup chicken broth
1/4 cup heavy cream
Chopped parsley

method

Pound the chicken breasts to form thin cutlets. Combine the thyme, salt, pepper and flour in a mixing bowl and dredge each chicken breast in the flour mixture. Shake off any excess flour. Heat the butter and oil in a large sauté pan. Place the floured chicken breasts in the pan and brown them on both sides. Remove the chicken from the pan and set aside.

To the same pan, add the butter and mushrooms over high heat and sauté for 2 minutes or until golden. Add the white wine and chicken stock, bring to a simmer and cook for 1 minute. Add the heavy cream and return the chicken to the pan. Cook for 2 minutes more, or until the chicken is heated through and the sauce has thickened slightly. Serve the chicken garnished with parsley.

SPANISH CHICKEN with RICE

Serves 6

intro

One of the most beloved dishes of Spain! The piquillo peppers, saffron and smoked paprika add an unmistakable Spanish touch and gorgeous color to the rice. Use short-grained Valencia-style rice-the same as used for Paella-or use Italian Arborio rice as a good substitute. I recommend pairing this dish with a hearty Spanish Rioja or California Zinfandel.

ingredients

One 4-pound chicken, cut into 8 pieces
6 tablespoons extra virgin olive oil
1 yellow onion, finely chopped
6 garlic cloves, minced
Salt and freshly ground pepper
6 tablespoons freshly chopped parsley
1/2 cup roasted piquillo peppers, cut into thin strips
1 teaspoon smoked paprika
1 pinch of saffron
3 1/2 cups chicken broth
1/2 cup dry white wine
2 cups Valencia or Arborio rice

method

Season the chicken with salt and pepper. In a large, deep pan heat the oil and sauté the chicken until golden on all sides. Remove the chicken to a plate and set aside. Add the onion, garlic and parsley to the pot and sauté until the onion is tender, about 5 minutes. Add the piquillo peppers, smoked paprika, saffron, broth, and wine and bring the mixture to a boil. Add the rice and cook over medium high heat, uncovered, for about 20 minutes, stirring until the rice is semi-dry but some liquid remains.

continued on next page

SPANISH CHICKEN with RICE

continued

Bury the chicken in the rice, then cover the pot and cook over low heat for 20 minutes. Turn the rice and the chicken over with a fork from bottom to top then replace the cover and simmer for another 10 minutes. Transfer the rice and chicken to a serving platter and garnish with chopped parsley.

chef's tip

Piquillo peppers have a rich, sweet flavor and emit only a minimal trace of heat. They are grown in Northern Spain and have a short plump shape with a tapered point (piquillo is Spanish for "little beak"). After being hand picked, they are roasted over an open fire, then peeled and packed in jars or tins. They are delicious served stuffed with goat cheese or tuna as a "tapas" and they add a wonderful hearty flavor to soups and sauces.

RASPBERRY MARINATED BAKED CHICKEN

Serves 4

intro

The raspberry jam, honey and soy sauce in this dish create an incredibly rich glaze for the chicken, both in taste and color. The Dijon mustard and garlic balance the sweet jam, so each bite is a mix of sweet and savory. This dish is particularly pretty accompanied by a green salad or vegetables to bring out the color of the wine and raspberry-tinted chicken. After one taste, you'll be stocking up on raspberry jam!

ingredients

1/2 cup dry red wine
1/2 cup raspberry vinegar
1 cup raspberry jam
2 tablespoons soy sauce
3 tablespoons honey
1 teaspoon Dijon mustard
1 garlic clove, minced
One 3-pound chicken, cut into pieces
Chopped parsley, for garnish

method

Mix together the wine, vinegar, jam, soy sauce, honey, Dijon and garlic and stir until well combined. Taste and adjust the sweetness to your personal preference. Pour the mixture over the chicken pieces and marinate for at least 4 hours (preferably overnight) in the refrigerator.

Preheat the oven to 375°F. Place the chicken pieces, with the marinade, in a large baking pan. Bake the chicken for 45 minutes, or until cooked through. Garnish with parsley and serve.

CHICKEN BRUSCHETTA

Serves 6

intro

One of my most requested recipes, this simple chicken dish comes alive with flavor from the tangy garlic and fresh tomato sauce. Serve the dish over creamy Parmesan Polenta or atop mashed potatoes for a hearty, comforting meal.

ingredients

1 cup all-purpose flour
3 eggs, slightly beaten
2 cups seasoned breadcrumbs
1/2 cup grated Parmesan cheese
6 boneless skinless chicken breasts
3 tablespoons unsalted butter
5 tablespoons extra-virgin olive oil
2 garlic cloves, minced
4 roma tomatoes, seeded and chopped
1/2 cup sun dried tomatoes packed in oil, drained
3 tablespoons fresh basil, cut into thin strips
Salt and freshly ground pepper

method

Place the flour and beaten eggs in separate shallow bowls, large enough to accommodate a chicken breast. In a third bowl combine the breadcrumbs and Parmesan cheese and set the three bowls up to form an assembly line.

Dredge each chicken breast in flour, then coat with the beaten egg, then coat each chicken breast in the breadcrumb mixture, shaking off any excess.

Heat the butter with 3 tablespoons of the olive oil in a large sauté pan over medium heat. Add the chicken breasts and sauté until golden brown on both sides and cooked through. Remove the chicken from the pan and keep warm. To the same pan, add the remaining 2 tablespoons of olive oil. Add the garlic and sauté 2 minutes. Add the fresh tomatoes, sun dried tomatoes and the basil and sauté 3 minutes, stirring often. Season the sauce with salt and pepper. Pour the sauce over the chicken and serve.

LANA'S CHICKEN CACCIATORE

Serves 6

intro

Cacciatore is Italian for "hunter", referring to a one-pot dish prepared "hunter style" with lots of hearty ingredients. This traditional, rustic dish has been handed down in my family over many generations. I love to serve it for friends over noodles, on top of rice or with soft, creamy polenta and we make this dish often, because it's Lana's favorite comfort food!

ingredients

1/2 cup all-purpose flour
Salt and pepper, to taste
One 4-pound fryer chicken, cut into pieces
6 tablespoons extra-virgin olive oil
2 yellow onions, sliced
2 garlic cloves, minced
1/2 teaspoon dried crushed red pepper flakes
1 pound sliced crimini or white mushrooms
1/2 cup dry red wine
2 cups tomato sauce
1 cup beef or chicken broth
2 tablespoons fresh basil, chopped
1 teaspoon fresh oregano, chopped
1/2 cup fresh parsley, chopped

method

Place the flour in a mixing bowl and season with salt and pepper. Dredge each piece of chicken in the flour and shake off any excess.

In a large, deep pot heat 4 tablespoons of the oil until very hot. Add the floured chicken pieces and brown the chicken on all sides. Remove the chicken from the pan and set aside.

Add the remaining oil to the pan along with the onions. Sauté until tender, about 8 minutes. Add the garlic, red pepper flakes and mushrooms and sauté 2 minutes more. Add the red wine and stir to combine, scraping any browned bits from the bottom of the pan. Add the tomatoes, tomato sauce, basil and oregano and stir to combine well. Return the chicken to the pot and cook covered, for 1 hour. Adjust the seasoning before serving. Garnish with chopped parsley.

ASIAN TURKEY BURGERS

Serves 8

intro

Fresh ginger and garlic give these burgers a pungent burst of flavor and the hoisin sauce keeps them moist while cooking. Serve a "burger buffet" with all the fixings needed for your guests to assemble their own piled-high masterpiece, with sweet onion slices, spreads and fresh-baked rolls. Offer sweet potato fries with sea salt and an Asian slaw as accompaniments.

ingredients

2 pounds lean ground turkey breast
1/2 cup seasoned breadcrumbs
4 tablespoons hoisin sauce
3 green onions, minced
2 tablespoons freshly grated ginger
2 garlic cloves, minced
Salt and freshly ground pepper
3 teaspoons sesame oil

Sesame Mayonnaise:
1 1/2 cups mayonnaise
1 teaspoon sesame oil
Salt and freshly ground pepper

method

Combine the ground turkey, bread crumbs, hoisin sauce, scallions, ginger, garlic and seasoning and mix well.

Divide the mixture into eight equal portions. Form the meat into 1/2-inch thick patties and refrigerate until ready to cook.

Heat your barbeque, stovetop grill or a large skillet to medium-high. Oil the grill or pour 2 tablespoons of olive oil into the sauté pan. Brush the patties with the sesame oil and grill or sauté until golden brown on both sides and cooked through (a thermometer inserted in the center of the burger should read 165°F), about 5 minutes per side.

To make the Sesame Mayonnaise, combine the mayonnaise with the sesame oil, salt and pepper and whisk to combine. Serve with the burgers.

TURKEY POT PIE

Serves 6

intro

Pot pie is a great way to use up leftover roasted turkey and this turkey pot pie presents beautifully on your "day after" buffet. It is the true definition of comfort food, but the puff pastry dresses it up into something special enough for entertaining.

ingredients

2 tablespoons extra-virgin olive oil
2 tablespoons unsalted butter
1 yellow onion, diced
2 carrots, peeled and diced
6 tablespoons all-purpose flour
4 cups hot chicken broth
Salt and freshly ground pepper
Tabasco sauce
2 Yukon Gold potatoes - peeled, cooked and diced
4 cups turkey, cooked and diced
1 cup sweet peas, fresh or frozen
1 sheet frozen Puff Pastry, thawed
1 egg, beaten

method

For the filling, heat the oil and butter in a large sauté pan over medium heat. Add the onion and carrot and sauté until tender, stirring often, about 10 minutes. Add the flour and mix well. Add the heated broth, slowly, whisking to dissolve the flour. When smooth, let the mixture simmer for 1 to 2 minutes to thicken. Stir in the cooked potatoes, turkey and peas and stir to combine. Season with salt, pepper and Tabasco and remove the pan from the heat. Set aside.

Preheat the oven to 375°F. Butter a large casserole. Roll out the thawed puff pastry on a lightly floured work surface, just enough to smooth out the creases. Cut the pastry to fit the top of the casserole, allowing for a 1-inch overhang. Transfer the puff pastry to a baking sheet and chill for 10 minutes.

Pour the filling into the buttered casserole. Top with the chilled puff pastry, pressing the overhang to the sides of the casserole. Brush the top of the pastry with the beaten egg and cut a slit in the top of the pastry to allow the steam to escape. Bake until puffed and golden, about 30 minutes.

Beef, Pork and Lamb Dishes

Meatball Heroes

Individual Meatloaves with Pan Gravy

Beer Braised Beef Stew

Classic Beef Stroganoff

Traditional English Roast Beef

Apple Stuffed Pork Loin
with Apple-Shallot Cream Sauce

Baby Back Ribs with Espresso Barbecue Sauce

Smothered Pork Chops with Apricots and Prunes

Braised Lamb Shanks in Red Wine

Irish Lamb Stew

MEATBALL HEROES

Serves 8

intro

Meatballs are made in every country and culture in the world. And, no wonder…They're easy to eat, pack a lot of flavor into a small bite, and are great for serving up a hungry crowd This recipe uses classic Italian seasonings and a rich marinara sauce for an absolutely mouth-watering hero sandwich.

ingredients

For the Meatballs:
1/2 pound ground beef
1/2 pound ground pork
3 garlic cloves, minced
1/2 yellow onion, diced
1 large egg
2/3 cup grated Parmesan cheese
1/4 cup dried Italian-style bread crumbs
1/4 cup freshly chopped parsley
1 teaspoon salt and 1 teaspoon freshly ground pepper
1/4 cup cold water
1/2 cup extra-virgin olive oil
3 cups store-bought or homemade Marinara

For the Sandwiches:
12 Italian rolls, split,
1/3 cup freshly grated Parmesan cheese

Method

To make the meatballs, combine the beef, pork, garlic, onion, egg, Parmesan, bread crumbs, parsley and salt and pepper in a large mixing bowl Add the cold water and mix to combine; Do not over mix. Shape the mixture into 1 1/2-inch-diameter meatballs.

Heat the oil in large frying pan over medium-high heat. Working in batches, add the meatballs and sauté until browned on all sides, about 5 minutes. Using a slotted spoon, transfer the meatballs to a plate. Pour off any excess oil. Return all the meatballs to the pan. Add the marinara sauce and simmer over low until the sauce thickens slightly and the flavors meld, about 10 minutes. Season the sauce with salt and pepper.

To assemble the sandwiches, spoon the hot meatballs with sauce over the bottoms of the rolls. Sprinkle with the Parmesan and serve.

INDIVIDUAL MEATLOAVES
with PAN GRAVY

Serves 4

intro

What is more homey and delicious than a thick slice of meatloaf with gravy, atop a pile of buttery, hot mashed potatoes? Even better, how about your own personal meatloaf? Delicious with each savory forkful.

ingredients

For the Meatloaf Patties:
2 slices white bread
1/4 cup heavy cream or milk
1 pound ground chuck
1/2 pound ground sirloin
1/4 cup yellow onion, finely grated minced
1 egg
2 tablespoons ketchup
1/2 teaspoon cumin
1 teaspoon Worcestershire sauce
Pinch of cayenne pepper
4 tablespoons olive oil
Salt and pepper, to taste

For the Gravy:
2 tablespoons unsalted butter
2 shallots, minced
2 tablespoons all-purpose flour
1 to 1 1/2 cups beef broth
1 teaspoon Dijon mustard
2 tablespoons fresh parsley, chopped
Salt and pepper, to taste

method

In a large mixing bowl combine the bread slices and cream or milk and allow the bread to soak up the liquid. Add the ground chuck, ground sirloin, onion, egg, ketchup, cumin, Worcestershire, cayenne and salt and pepper. Using your hands, mix to combine the ingredients, but do not over mix.

Form the mixture into 4 large oval patties, about 3/4-inch thick. Heat the olive oil in a large sauté pan. Add the meatloaf patties and pan fry until golden and cooked through, about 7 minutes per side.

continued on next page

INDIVIDUAL MEATLOAVES
with PAN GRAVY

Continued

Remove the meat loaf patties to a platter and return the pan to the heat. Reduce the heat to medium and add the butter and shallots to the pan. Cook the shallots for 2-3 minutes, or until tender, then sprinkle with flour. Cook the mixture for 1 minute while stirring, then whisk in 1 cup of beef stock. Bring the gravy to a simmer to thicken. If the gravy is too thick, thin it with the additional stock. Stir in the mustard and parsley. Return the individual meatloaves to the pan to re-warm and coat with the gravy. Serve over mashed potatoes.

BEER BRAISED BEEF STEW

Serves 6

intro

Turning a tough cut of meat into a hearty, succulent meal involves only a couple of hours of slow simmering. Many recipes call for a simple stock or red wine, which not only braises the meat but also imparts a flavor and, in turn, thickens and reduces into the perfect accompanying sauce. This recipe uses Belgian-style ale, which enhances the simple, earthy taste of the beef and sautéed onions. Like a Pot Roast, only better!

ingredients

1/4 pound thick-cut bacon, cut into 1/2-inch pieces
3 pounds beef chuck or round, cut into large chunks
Salt and freshly ground black pepper
2 to 3 tablespoons olive oil
2 large onions, thinly sliced
2 (12-ounce) bottles ale
2 tablespoons all-purpose flour
4 sprigs fresh thyme
3 sprigs fresh flat-leaf parsley
3 dried bay leaves
6 carrots, peeled and cut into 2-inch chunks
4 parsnips, peeled and cut into 2-inch chunks
1 cup frozen pearl onions, thawed

method

Preheat oven to 325°F. In a medium-large Dutch oven, cook the bacon over medium-low heat until crisp, stirring frequently, about 10 minutes. Transfer to a paper-towel-lined baking sheet; set aside.

Season the flour with salt and pepper and dredge the cubed meat in the seasoned flour, shaking off any excess. Add 2 tablespoons of oil to the pot, and raise heat to medium high. Working in batches, sear the meat until golden brown all over. As each batch is browned, transfer the meat to a plate and set aside.

Lower the heat to medium. Add the onions and sauté 3 minutes. Create a Bouquet Garni by tying the thyme, parsley, and bay leaves in a bundle with a piece of kitchen twine. Add the bouquet garni to the onions and return the bacon and browned beef to the pot. Add the ale and bring to a simmer, scraping any browned bits from the bottom of the pan. Cover the pot and transfer it to the oven. Cook until beef is fork tender, about 2 hours.   During the last half-hour of cooking, add the carrot and parsnip chunks along with the pearl onions. To serve, remove the herb bundle and discard and adjust the seasoning.

CLASSIC BEEF STROGANOFF

Serves 6

intro

Stroganoff's rich beef base with a topping of cream originated in 19th century Russia. The beefy broth with caramelized onions has both a little heat from the red pepper flakes and a little zing from the lemon zest. I love it served on a bed of buttered egg noodles.

ingredients

1 cup all-purpose flour
Salt and freshly ground pepper
2 1/2 pounds round or chuck beef, cut into 2-inch cubes
4 tablespoons butter
2 tablespoons olive oil
2 yellow, onions, thinly sliced
1/2 teaspoon red pepper flakes
1 bay leaf
Zest of 1 lemon
1 cup beef broth
1 pound mushrooms, sliced
3/4 cup crème fraiche or sour cream

method

Place the flour in a mixing bowl and season it with salt and pepper. Dredge the beef cubes in the flour to coat well and shake off any excess. In a large, heavy skillet heat 3 tablespoons of the butter with the oil until hot. Add the beef and brown on all sides over high heat. Remove the meat from the pan, using a slotted spoon and set aside. To the same pan, add the onions and red pepper flakes and sauté about 5 minutes to wilt the onions. Return the browned beef to the pan along with the bay leaf, lemon zest and beef broth. Bring the mixture to a slow simmer, then cover the pan tightly and place over the lowest heat possible. Cook for 1 hour, stirring often.

continued on next page

CLASSIC BEEF STROGANOFF

Continued

In a separate pan, heat the remaining 1 tablespoon of butter. Add the mushrooms and sauté the mushrooms until wilted. Add the mushrooms and their juices to the meat mixture and mix well. Remove the bay leaf from the pot and discard. Add the crème fraiche and cook the stroganoff for 5 minutes more. If the stroganoff seems too thick, thin with hot beef stock to the desired consistency. Serve the stroganoff on top of buttered egg noodles.

chef's tip

Crème Fraiche is a French-style thickened cream with a slightly tangy flavor and an incredibly rich texture. It is the ideal addition to sauces or soups because it can be boiled without curdling and it makes a delicious accompaniment to fresh fruit or on top of desserts, in place of whipped cream. You can buy it in the cheese section of most markets.

TRADITIONAL ENGLISH ROAST BEEF

Serves 8 to 10

intro

This is THE best Roast Beef you have ever tasted! Perfect on a buffet with mashed potatoes, glazed carrots, Brussels sprouts with bacon and a traditional English mustard or horseradish.

ingredients

7 to 8 pound Standing rib roast with three to four ribs, trimmed
2 teaspoons dry mustard
2 teaspoons Dijon mustard
2 tablespoons granulated sugar
Kosher salt and freshly ground black pepper
Caramelized juices from the roasting pan
2 tablespoons all-purpose flour
2 cups beef broth

method

Combine the dry mustard, sugar, and Dijon mustard in a small mixing bowl and rub the mixture over the fat side and the cut surfaces of the roast. Refrigerate the roast at least 2 hours or overnight.

Preheat the oven to 450°F. Set the roast, rib side down, in a heavy, shallow roasting pan. Sprinkle the roast liberally with salt and pepper.

Roast the beef for 15 minutes at 450ºF, then lower the oven to 350° and continue roasting the meat, basting every 15 minutes, until cooked to the desired temperature.

For Rare: 12 to 15 minutes per pound and 125° to 130°F internal temperature
For Medium: 15 to 18 minutes per pound and 140° to 145°
For Well Done: 18 to 20 minutes per pound and 160° to 165°F

Remove the roast from the pan and transfer to a platter. Tent the roast with aluminum foil and let it rest for 15 minutes before carving.

continued on next page

TRADITIONAL ENGLISH ROAST BEEF

Continued

For the gravy, pour off all but 2 tablespoons of the fat from the roasting pan, leaving the caramelized browned bits on the bottom of the pan. Set the roasting pan on the stove over medium heat and stir in the flour.   Scrape up the browned bits from the bottom of the pan and cook the flour until golden brown, about 2 minutes. Add the beef broth and whisk to create a smooth gravy. Bring the gravy to a boil, stirring until it thickens. Adjust the seasoning, slice the roast and serve.

APPLE STUFFED PORK LOIN with APPLE-SHALLOT CREAM SAUCE

Serves 6 to 8

intro

This recipe is my take on the traditional pork and applesauce combination I grew up eating (a perfect pairing!). The apples and onions roast together in a stuffing that keeps the pork loin moist, while the cream sauce adds another rich layer to the sweet and savory combination.

ingredients

For the Pork Loin:
One 3-pound pork loin, deboned and left untied
Salt and freshly ground pepper
2 Braeburn, Macintosh or Granny Smith apples, sliced
1 small yellow onion, sliced
1 teaspoon fresh thyme leaves, chopped
1/2 cup chicken broth

For the Apple-Shallot Cream Sauce:
2 tablespoons unsalted butter
2 tablespoons shallots, minced
1 green apple, peeled and diced
1 cup chicken broth
1 cup heavy cream

method

Preheat the oven to 400°F.

Lay the pork loin flat on a work surface and season with salt and pepper. Arrange the apple and onion slices, lengthwise, down the center of the roast. Bring the sides of the roast together to enclose the apple and onion, then roll the loin to enclose the filling and form a rolled roast. Tie the loin with kitchen twine in several places to hold the roast together. Season the outside of the roast with salt, pepper and thyme.

continued on next page

APPLE STUFFED PORK LOIN with APPLE-SHALLOT CREAM SAUCE

Continued

Pour the chicken broth in the bottom of a roasting pan. Set the roast on a rack in the pan and place the pan in the preheated oven. Immediately turn the oven down to 350°F and roast for 1 hour to 1 hour and 15 minutes, or until the pork reaches an internal temperature of 140-145°F.

For the Apple-Shallot Cream Sauce, heat the butter in a saucepan over medium heat. Add the shallots and apple and sauté for 5 minutes. Add the chicken broth and bring to a boil. Stir well, then set the sauce aside.

When the roast is done, remove it from the roasting pan to allow the roast to rest before carving. Place the roasting pan on top of the stove, over medium heat and add the prepared sauce to the roasting pan. Deglaze the pan with the sauce, scraping up any browned bits from the bottom of the roasting pan. Simmer for 5 minutes. Add the cream, reduce the heat to low and simmer gently for 5 minutes more. Serve the sauce with the pork loin.

BABY BACK RIBS with ESPRESSO BARBECUE SAUCE

Serves 6

intro

Espresso combined with balsamic vinegar and soy sauce, makes a barbecue sauce that is decadently rich! You can precook the ribs and the barbecue sauce, until you're ready to fire up the grill. The sauce will create a gorgeous dark glaze on the ribs…be sure to make extra for dipping! (Yes, it is that good!)

ingredients

3 racks baby back ribs
Salt and freshly ground black pepper, to taste
2 tablespoons extra-virgin olive oil
3 garlic cloves, minced
1 cup honey
1 cup ketchup
1/2 cup balsamic vinegar
1/4 cup brewed espresso or strong coffee
1/4 cup soy sauce

method

Preheat the oven to 325°F.

Cut each rack of ribs in half. Season each rack on both sides with salt and pepper or your favorite Chef Jamie Spice Rub. Stack the ribs in a roasting pan or on a foil covered baking sheet, in two piles of three pieces each and cover the pan tightly with aluminum foil. Bake for 1 1/2 hours.

For the sauce, in a medium saucepan heat the olive oil and add the garlic. Sauté 1 minute or until just golden. Add the honey, ketchup, vinegar, espresso and soy sauce. Bring the sauce to a simmer and cook for 15 minutes to blend the flavors.

To finish the ribs, preheat your barbecue or stovetop grill to high. Brush the Espresso BBQ Sauce on both sides of the ribs and grill until the ribs are glazed, about 10 minutes, turning once and basting often.

Serve the extra sauce with the ribs, for dipping.

SMOTHERED PORK CHOPS
with APRICOTS and PRUNES

Serves 4

intro

The sweet and savory blend of flavors in this recipe elevates pork chops to a whole new level and the dried apricots and prunes saturated with red wine create a rich and colorful dish. Serve the chops with a fruity Zinfandel.

ingredients

6 double-cut pork chops
1 cup all-purpose flour
3 tablespoons olive oil
2 tablespoons unsalted butter
2 yellow onions, sliced thinly
1 cup dry red wine
3 cups chicken broth
1 cup dried apricots
1 cup pitted prunes
Salt and freshly ground pepper

method

Trim the pork chops of any excess fat. Place the flour in a shallow bowl and season it liberally with salt and pepper. Coat each pork chop with the flour and shake off any excess.

Heat the oil and butter in a large high-sided sauté pan. Brown the pork chops on both sides over high heat, then transfer the chops to a plate and set them aside.

Remove all but 2 tablespoons of the fat from the pan. Add the onions to the pan and sauté over medium heat until golden and tender, stirring often, about 15 minutes. Add the wine and deglaze the pan, scraping up any browned bits from the bottom of the pan. Add the stock, prunes and apricots to the pan and place the browned pork chops back in the pan. Bring the pot to a simmer, reduce the heat to low and cover the pan. Allow the pork to cook over low heat for 1 hour.

Serve the pork chops with the sauce and fruit.

BRAISED LAMB SHANKS in RED WINE

Serves 8

intro

Braising is a cooking method somewhat like stewing, but it requires less liquid and a longer cooking time. The result is tender, fall-off-the-bone meat that has been infused with the flavors of the braising liquid. Small lamb shanks are mainly bone, so be sure to buy the largest, meatiest shanks you can find. This is a great dinner to make in cooler weather, as it warms up the house with its delectable aroma.

ingredients

1 bottle dry red wine
1/4 cup olive oil
8 lamb shanks
1 cup all-purpose flour
2 yellow onions, sliced
4 garlic cloves, minced
1/4 cup tomato paste
Two (15 1/2-ounce) cans beef broth
1 tablespoon red wine vinegar
3 tablespoons brown sugar
Juice of half a lemon
1 tablespoon Worcestershire sauce
1 bay leaf
3 sprigs fresh rosemary
1/2 cup freshly chopped parsley, for garnish
Salt and freshly ground pepper

method

Preheat the oven to 325°F.

Pour the entire bottle of wine into a medium saucepot and bring to a boil. Reduce the heat and simmer until the wine is reduced by half.

In a large pot, heat the oil. Season the lamb shanks with salt and pepper and dust each shank with flour to coat. Add the shanks to the pan and brown well on all sides. Remove the shanks from the pan.

continued on next page

BRAISED LAMB SHANKS in RED WINE

Continued

Add the onions and garlic to the same pot and sauté until tender. Add the reduced wine, ketchup, broth, vinegar, brown sugar, lemon juice, Worcestershire, bay leaf and rosemary and stir to combine well. Add the lamb shanks back to the pot and bring the mixture to a simmer. Cover the pot and place it in the oven. Bake for 2 hours or until the lamb is very tender and falling off the bone.

Before serving, adjust the seasoning. Serve the shanks with the sauce, garnished with chopped parsley.

chef's tip

The lamb shanks are best made a day before serving, so that you can skim the fat from the cold pot before rewarming the shanks. Rewarm the shanks, covered, over low heat before serving. A serious Italian red wine will be the perfect compliment.

IRISH LAMB STEW

Serves 6

intro

Filled with tender vegetables and, of course, potatoes, this Irish lamb stew is a complete meal in a pot. Enriched with red wine and beef broth, the lamb simmers into a flavorful stew, perfumed with fresh rosemary sprigs. It's an Irish stew, so it's meant to be paired with a frosty glass of dark ale and some extra bread for dipping.

ingredients

3 pounds boneless leg of lamb, trimmed and cut into 1 1/2-inch cubes
1/2 cup all-purpose flour
Salt and freshly ground black pepper
2 tablespoons extra-virgin olive oil
3 garlic cloves, finely chopped
1 1/2 cups dry red wine
3 cups beef broth
1 (15-ounce) can diced tomatoes in juice
1 tablespoon tomato paste
2 sprigs fresh rosemary
12 small potatoes, halved
2 large carrots, peeled and cut into 1-inch pieces
1/2 pound sliced baby portabella or crimini mushrooms

method

Place the flour in a shallow bowl and season liberally with salt and pepper. Dredge the lamb cubes in the flour to coat, shaking off any excess.

Heat the olive oil over medium-high heat in a large pot and brown the lamb cubes all over. Remove the lamb from the pot and set it aside.

To the same pot, add the garlic and sauté 1 minute. Add the wine and simmer over medium heat until the wine is reduced by half. Return the lamb to the pot along with the broth, tomatoes with their juices, tomato paste and the rosemary sprigs. Scrape up any caramelized bits from the bottom of the pot. Partially cover the pot and simmer over medium-low heat until the lamb is tender, about 45 minutes.

Add the potatoes, carrots and mushrooms to the stew and simmer 30 minutes longer, or until the vegetables are tender. Adjust the seasoning and serve.

Everyday Pastas

Bacon Mac and Cheese

Baked Penne with Chicken Sausage
and Three Cheeses

Penne with Tequila Clam Sauce

Spaghetti with Easy Italian Meat Sauce

Fusilli with Bacon, Mushrooms,
Asparagus and Cherry Tomatoes

Penne Puttanesca

Fettuccini Gorgonzola

Warm Antipasto Pasta Salad

Cold Sesame Noodles

BACON MAC and CHEESE

Serves 6

intro

What could be better than creamy Mac and Cheese?...Bacon Mac and Cheese! This stove top version uses the bacon drippings to make the cheese sauce, infusing it with a wonderful, smoky flavor. We recommend a sharp cheddar cheese, as it holds its own with the salty, rich bacon. If you're looking for a new pasta choice try cavatappi, which looks like a spiral-shaped elbow macaroni.

ingredients

8 slices thick-cut bacon, cut into 2-inch pieces
1 pound elbow macaroni
2 tablespoons all purpose flour
1 1/2 cups whole milk
1/2 teaspoon hot sauce
1/2 teaspoon dry mustard
Salt and freshly ground white pepper
3 cups grated sharp cheddar cheese (about 12 ounces)

method

Cook the pasta in a large pot of salted boiling water then drain the pasta and set it aside.

Cook the bacon in a large skillet over medium heat, stirring occasionally, until browned and crisp. Using a slotted spoon, remove the bacon to a paper towel-lined plate to drain. Discard all but two tablespoons of the bacon grease. Place the pan with the bacon grease back on the stove over low heat and stir in the flour. Cook 1 minute. Gradually whisk in the milk and season with hot sauce, dry mustard, salt and pepper. Cook until the sauce is smooth and slightly thickened, whisking constantly, about 3 minutes. Add the cheese and stir until the cheese melts completely. Stir in the cooked macaroni and cook 3 minutes, or until heated through.

Stir in the bacon and serve immediately.

BAKED ZITI with CHICKEN SAUSAGE & THREE CHEESES

Serves 4

intro

Hearty and full of flavor, this pasta dish has a rich sauce featuring vodka and cream and the blend of three cheeses makes it even more delicious. Colorful and satisfying, baked ziti with chicken sausage is the perfect buffet and potluck dish.

ingredients

2 tablespoons extra virgin olive oil
1 medium red onion, diced
4 garlic cloves, minced
1/4 cup Vodka
1 28-ounce diced tomatoes in puree
1 teaspoon dried oregano
1/2 cup heavy cream
Salt & pepper, to taste
1 pound ziti pasta
2 cups baby spinach leaves
1 pound smoked chicken sausage, cut lengthwise & sliced 1/4-inch thick
1/2 cup shredded mozzarella cheese
1/2 cup shredded fontina cheese
1/4 cup grated Parmesan cheese

method

Heat the oil in a large skillet over medium heat. Add the onion and sauté until golden and tender, about 10 minutes. Add the garlic and sauté 1 minute more. Remove the pan from the heat add the vodka. Return the pan to the heat and cook until the vodka is almost evaporated, about 1 minute. Stir in the tomatoes and oregano and cook 10 minutes. Add the cream and simmer 5 minutes. Season with salt and pepper.

Meanwhile, preheat the oven to 400°F. Cook the ziti in a large pot of salted boiling water. Drain the pasta well and add the spinach to the drained pasta to wilt it slightly. Add the pasta to the pan of sauce, along with the sausage, and toss to combine.

Combine the mozzarella, fontina and parmesan in a mixing bowl. Place half of the pasta mixture in a baking dish and top with half of the cheese. Top with the remaining pasta, then finish with the remaining shredded cheese.

Bake 25 minutes or until the cheese is melted and the edges of the baked pasta are crisp.

LINGUINE with TEQUILA CLAM SAUCE

Serves 6

intro

Clam juice, jarred chopped clams and penne pasta can be kept in the pantry, so you can make this dish at a moment's notice. Serve this delectable dish with crusty garlic bread and a crisp Sauvignon Blanc.

ingredients

1 pound linguine
2 tablespoons extra virgin olive oil
1/2 teaspoon crushed red pepper flakes
1/4 cup yellow onion, diced
2 garlic cloves, minced
1 tablespoon fresh thyme, chopped
1/2 cup white wine
1 cup clam juice
1 cup chopped clams
Freshly ground pepper
4 tablespoons chilled butter, cut into small pieces
1/4 cup Tequila
1/4 cup parsley, chopped

method

Cook the pasta in a large pot of salted boiling water then drain and set aside.

Heat the olive oil over medium heat in a large sauté pan. Sauté the onion until tender and translucent, stirring often, about 10 minutes. Add the garlic and red pepper flakes and sauté 1 minute more. Add the thyme leaves, white wine and clam juice and cook for 3 minutes. Add the chopped clams and pepper. Remove the pan from the heat and add the butter, a little at a time, swirling the pan to incorporate the butter. Return the pan to the heat and add the tequila. Cook the sauce for 30 seconds more. Stir the parsley into the sauce. Toss the sauce with the cooked pasta and serve.

FUSILLI with BACON, MUSHROOMS, ASPARAGUS and CHERRY TOMATOES

Serves 6

intro

Fusilli—or "twisted spaghetti"—is a large, spiral shaped pasta that holds onto sauce wonderfully. The combination of grated Parmesan, with a little olive oil and bacon drippings cling to every noodle. This is the perfect pasta dish to welcome the first asparagus of spring!

ingredients

6 slices thick-cut bacon, cut into 1/2-inch pieces
2 tablespoons extra-virgin olive oil
3 garlic cloves, minced
1 bunch asparagus, cut into 1-inch pieces
2 cups sliced brown mushrooms
1 pound fusilli
1/2 cup finely grated Parmesan cheese
Salt and freshly ground pepper

method

Cook the bacon in a large skillet over medium heat, stirring occasionally, until browned and crisp. Add the garlic, mushrooms and asparagus to the skillet and cook, stirring occasionally, about 3 minutes. Add the tomatoes and cooked pasta and toss well. Serve garnished with freshly grated Parmesan Cheese.

SPAGHETTI and EASY ITALIAN MEAT SAUCE

Serves 6

intro

Rather than the typical marinara sauce, try this version of a meaty tomato sauce that doesn't need to cook for long. The addition of milk might seem unusual, but it's traditional in northern Italy and it creates a sauce with gorgeous color.

ingredients

2 tablespoons unsalted butter
2 tablespoons olive oil
1 carrot, grated
1 onion, chopped
2 garlic cloves, chopped
3/4 pound ground beef
1 28-ounce can whole tomatoes
1/2 cup milk
1 dried bay leaf
1/2 teaspoon dried thyme
1/4 teaspoon ground nutmeg
Salt and freshly ground pepper
1 pound spaghetti
Grated Parmesan cheese, for serving

method

Heat the butter and oil in a large pan over medium heat. Stir in the carrot, onion, and garlic. Add the ground beef and cook through, stirring often, about 5 minutes.

Add the tomatoes and their liquid, crushing them with the back of a large spoon. Stir in the milk, bay leaf, thyme, nutmeg, salt and pepper. Simmer the sauce for 20 minutes.

Cook the spaghetti in a large pot of salted boiling water then drain well, reserving 1/2 cup of the cooking water from the pasta pot. Return the pasta to the warm pot. Add the meat sauce and toss to combine. Add the pasta water, as needed, to loosen the sauce. Serve the pasta, garnished with Parmesan.

chef's tip

Reserving some of the pasta cooking water is ideal for adjusting the consistency of the sauce and the starch in the water helps the sauce adhere to the pasta.

PENNE PUTTANESCA

Serves 6

intro

The spicy combination of olives, capers, red pepper and fresh herbs make every bite of this spicy pasta a treat. Don't worry about the anchovy in the sauce's base; it simply melts away to create a nuttiness that adds to the dish's medley of flavors. Serve this pasta with a great Chianti.

ingredients

1/3 cup extra virgin olive oil
4 garlic cloves, thinly sliced
2 anchovy fillets
1/2 teaspoon hot red pepper flakes
1/4 cup chopped parsley
1/4 cup basil, cut into thin strips
1 12-oz. can diced tomatoes in puree
1/2 cup Kalamata olives
3 tablespoons capers, drained
Freshly ground pepper, to taste
1 pound penne pasta, cooked

method

Heat the oil in a large sauté pan heat the oil. Add the garlic and sauté over medium heat until tender and lightly golden. Add the anchovy fillets and stir to dissolve. Increase the heat and add the red pepper flakes, parsley, basil, tomatoes, olives and capers. Season with pepper and simmer for 10 minutes to blend the flavors.

While the sauce is cooking, cook the pasta in a large pot of salted boiling water and drain well. Toss the hot pasta with the prepared sauce and serve.

FETTUCCINE GORGONZOLA

Serves 4

intro

The toasted walnuts in this dish add crunch, while the fresh tomatoes enhance the pasta with aromatic flavors and colors...I simply love this combination! Paired with an endive salad and a bottle of Viognier, it's a heavenly meal!

ingredients

1 pound fettuccine
1 1/2 cups crumbled gorgonzola cheese
1 cup heavy whipping cream
3 tablespoons extra virgin olive oil
4 garlic cloves, minced
2 cups fresh tomatoes, seeded and chopped
1/2 cup fresh basil leaves, torn into pieces
1/2 cup walnuts, toasted and coarsely chopped
Salt and freshly ground white pepper
Freshly chopped parsley

method

Cook the fettuccine in a large pot of salted boiling water then drain well and set aside. In a small saucepan heat the cream until bubbles form around the edge of the pot, just before a simmer. Add the gorgonzola cheese and whisk over low heat to blend together. Season with salt and pepper. Remove the sauce from the stove and set aside.

Heat the olive oil n a large sauté pan over medium heat. Add the garlic and sauté for 1 minute. Add the tomatoes, basil and walnuts and sauté 1 minute more. Stir in the cream mixture. Add the hot pasta and toss to coat.

Serve immediately, garnished with freshly chopped parsley.

WARM ANTIPASTO PASTA SALAD

Serves 6

intro

I use fusilli in this salad, but any noodle that holds sauce will work well here. Since the dressing is made with mustard, wine and olive oil—and can be served warm or cold—this antipasto salad travels well and is ideal for a picnic.

ingredients

For the Dressing:
1 garlic clove
1 tablespoon Dijon mustard
3 tablespoons red-wine vinegar
1/3 cup extra-virgin olive oil
Salt and freshly ground pepper

For the Pasta Salad:
1 pound fusilli
1/2 pound smoked mozzarella cheese, cubed
One 14-ounce can garbanzo beans
1/2 pound sliced hard salami, cut into thin strips
1 red bell pepper, cut into 1-inch pieces
1 green bell pepper, cut into 1-inch pieces
3 tomatoes, seeded and chopped
1 tablespoon dried oregano
2 tablespoons freshly chopped parsley

1/4 cup freshly grated Parmesan cheese

method

Cook the pasta in a large pot of salted boiling water then drain well and set aside.

In a blender or food processor combine the garlic, mustard, and vinegar. With the blender running, slowly drizzle in the olive oil to form a thick dressing. Season with salt and pepper.

In a large mixing bowl combine the cooked pasta, mozzarella cheese, garbanzo beans, salami, bell peppers, tomatoes, oregano, parsley and Parmesan cheese.

Add the dressing and toss to coat well. Serve the pasta salad warm or cold.

COLD SESAME NOODLES

Serves 8

intro

I love these noodles served alongside citrus grilled chicken or seared tuna. And, they're perfect on a picnic or at an outdoor barbecue because they hold up beautifully. Make the dish the day before serving for the best flavor.

ingredients

8 ounces egg noodles
1/2 cup peanut butter
1/2 cup sesame paste
3 tablespoons canola oil
3/4 cup chicken broth
2 tablespoons freshly grated ginger
2 tablespoons champagne vinegar
2 tablespoons granulated sugar
3 tablespoons soy sauce
2 cups Napa cabbage, shredded
2 small or 1 large red bell pepper, cleaned and cut into thin strips
2 cups snow peas, cleaned and cut into thin strips
1/2 cup green onions, thinly sliced

method

Boil the noodles in a large pot of salted boiling water until soft. Drain the noodles and keep them warm.

In a large mixing bowl whisk together the peanut butter, sesame paste, chicken broth, ginger, vinegar, sugar and soy sauce. Combine until well blended.

Toss the warm noodles with the sauce. Stir in the cabbage, red bell peppers and snow peas. Garnish with green onions and serve.

Potatoes, Risotto, Rice and Polenta

Loaded Mashed Potato Casserole

Garlic Roasted Red Potatoes and Fennel

Caramelized Shallots, Parsnips and Potatoes

Spicy Sweet Potato Gratin

Warm Lemon Herb Potato Salad

Asparagus Risotto

Nutty Rice Pilaf

Toasted Rice with Piquillo Peppers
and Artichokes

Creamy Polenta with Crumbled Blue Cheese

LOADED MASHED POTATO CASSEROLE

Serves 8

intro

This is the mashed potato recipe of your dreams... the dish that friends and family will beg you to make. And, it's so easy! You can make this casserole lower in fat by substituting the low-fat version of the milk, sour cream and cream cheese.

ingredients

4 pounds baking potatoes, peeled and cut into large chunks
1/2 cup whole milk
One 8-ounce package cream cheese, softened
1 cup sour cream
1 cup shredded sharp cheddar cheese
12 slices thick-cut bacon, cooked and crumbled

method

Combine the potatoes with cold water in a large pot. Bring the water to a boil over medium-high heat, then reduce the heat to low and simmer until the potatoes are cooked through, about 15 minutes. Drain the potatoes well and puree them using a ricer or masher. Add the cream cheese and sour cream to the potatoes and blend well.

Preheat the oven to 350°F. Spoon half of the mixture into a lightly greased casserole and sprinkle with half of the shredded cheese. Top with the remaining mashed potato mixture and sprinkle the remaining cheese over top. Cover the casserole with a lid or aluminum foil and bake for 25 minutes. Remove the lid and sprinkle the cooked bacon over the top of the casserole. Bake 10 minutes longer or until heated through and bubbly.

GARLIC ROASTED RED POTATOES and FENNEL

Serves 6

intro

The aromatics and herbs in this recipe are what make this red potato dish distinctive. Fennel has a light anise flavor which brightens the dish, while the roasted garlic and rosemary have the savory tastes we crave.

ingredients

2 pounds baby red potatoes, scrubbed clean
2 fennel bulbs, cleaned and cut into 6 wedges each
3 tablespoons extra-virgin olive oil
12 garlic cloves, peeled
6 sprigs fresh rosemary
Salt and freshly ground pepper

method

Preheat the oven to 350°F. Place the potatoes in a large pot of cold water. Boil the potatoes until just tender, about 10 minutes after the boil begins. Drain the potatoes well and place them in a shallow roasting pan or on a baking sheet, along with the raw fennel wedges. Add the oil, garlic cloves, rosemary sprigs and toss to coat. Season liberally with salt and pepper. Bake for 30 minutes, tossing often, until golden.

CARAMELIZED SHALLOTS, PARSNIPS and POTATOES

Serves 6

intro

Parsnips, an unexpected and often neglected vegetable, truly shine when slow roasted. Serve this with grilled or roasted meats, or as a great brunch side dish with eggs.

ingredients

8 shallots, peeled and left whole
8 parsnips, peeled and cut into 2-inch pieces
12 small white potatoes, quartered
1/4 to 1/2 cup extra virgin olive oil
Salt and freshly ground pepper

method

Preheat the oven to 375°F. Combine the shallots, parsnips and quartered potatoes in a shallow casserole or on a baking sheet. Drizzle the vegetables with the olive oil and season liberally with salt and pepper. Toss to coat well. Roast the vegetables for 45 minutes, stirring often, or until the vegetables are caramelized and tender.

SPICY SWEET POTATO GRATIN

Serves 8

intro

Combining sweet potatoes with brown sugary goodness and a hint of spicy adobo will tickle your taste buds…And, the vibrant orange splash of color on your plate compliments any entrée. This dish compliments grilled pork, roast turkey, or even scallops beautifully.

ingredients

4 tablespoons unsalted butter, at room temperature
3 pounds sweet potatoes
3 garlic cloves, peeled and minced
Salt and freshly ground pepper
2 cups heavy whipping cream
1 tablespoon brown sugar
1 tablespoon adobo sauce from a can of chipotles in adobo

method

Preheat the oven to 350°F. Coat a large, shallow baking dish with 2 tablespoons of the butter. Place the remaining 2 tablespoons of butter in a small saucepan over medium heat. Add the garlic and sauté until tender, about 2 minutes, stirring often. Slowly add the whipping cream along with the brown sugar and adobo sauce. Bring the mixture to a simmer, then remove it from the heat.

Peel the sweet potatoes and slice them 1/4-inch thick, using a mandolin or sharp knife. Arrange the slices in overlapping layers in the prepared baking dish, and season each layer with salt and pepper.

Pour the cream mixture evenly over the potatoes, coating all exposed surfaces. Cover the dish tightly with foil and bake for 45 minutes. Remove the foil and bake uncovered until the top is golden brown, about 15 minutes more. Allow the gratin to cool for 10 minutes before serving.

chef's tip

Chipotle Chilies are dried, smoked jalapeños and they come canned in a spicy tomato sauce. They are available at most supermarkets and I love to use the sauce (be careful…the chilies are very hot!) for adding heat and smoky flavor to salad dressings, sauces, rice and more.

WARM LEMON HERB POTATO SALAD

Serves 8

intro

Potato salad is a traditional favorite for backyard barbecues and picnics…and my mayo-less and roasted version of potato salad is simply delicious! Adding the lemon dressing while the potatoes are warm helps the flavors meld together. Serve alongside grilled chicken or burgers and baked beans and enjoy!

ingredients

2 pounds Yukon Gold potatoes or new potatoes, cut into quarters
2 tablespoons + 2/3 cup extra-virgin olive oil
12 peeled garlic cloves, left whole
Zest of 1 lemon
1/4 cup fresh lemon juice
1/4 cup fresh tarragon, finely chopped
1/4 cup fresh basil, finely chopped
1/4 cup fresh mint, finely chopped
1 tablespoon Dijon mustard
1 cup small cherry tomatoes, halved
Salt and freshly ground pepper

method

Preheat the oven to 400°F. In a mixing bowl combine the potatoes with the garlic cloves and add a drizzle of olive oil to lightly coat. Season with salt and pepper. Arrange the potatoes on a baking sheet and roast for 30 minutes, stirring occasionally, until tender and golden. Keep warm.

In a small mixing bowl or using a blender, whisk together the lemon juice, fresh herbs and mustard. Slowly pour in the oil in a slow, steady stream to create an emulsified dressing. Season the dressing with salt and pepper.

Place the warm roasted potatoes and roasted garlic cloves in a serving bowl. Toss with enough dressing to coat well. Top with the halved cherry tomatoes and serve.

ASPARAGUS RISOTTO

Serves 6

intro

Parmesan cheese is a must for risotto, but it seems to have met its perfect match with asparagus, too! You'll need Arborio rice to achieve classic, creamy risotto. Arborio is a shorter, rounder grain that cooks up firm and buttery with a high starch content. The addition of sautéed asparagus makes this a great spring dish when fresh, tender asparagus start showing up at the farm stands. Pour a little extra white wine for the cook and your guests, and bring them into the kitchen with you to talk and enjoy the time-honored process of making the perfect risotto.

ingredients

5 to 6 cups chicken broth
4 tablespoons extra virgin olive oil
1 pound asparagus, cleaned and cut 1-inch pieces
1 small yellow onion, diced
2 garlic cloves, minced
1 1/2 cups Arborio rice
1 cup dry white wine
2 tablespoons butter
1/2 cup finely grated Parmesan cheese
Salt and Freshly ground pepper

method

Bring the chicken broth to a simmer in a saucepan.

In a large heavy pot, heat 2 tablespoons of the olive oil over high heat. Add the asparagus and sauté 2 minutes. Season with salt and pepper. Remove the asparagus from the pan and reserve.

Add the remaining 2 tablespoons of olive oil to the pan. Add the onion and garlic and cook until softened but not colored, about 2 minutes. Add the rice and stir to coat with the oil. Add the wine, bring to a simmer and stir constantly until the rice has absorbed the wine.

continued on next page

ASPARAGUS RISOTTO

Continued

Ladle 1/2 cup of hot chicken broth into the pan and stir until absorbed. Continue with the rest of the broth, adding 1/2 cup at a time and allowing each addition to be absorbed completely before adding more liquid. It will take about 30 minutes for the rice to cook through and become deliciously creamy. When ready to serve, fold in the reserved asparagus. Stir in the butter and the grated Parmesan and serve.

chef's tip

Make-Ahead Risotto, the restaurant way! Cook the risotto as suggested above, until 2/3 of the required liquid has been absorbed. Remove the risotto from the heat and spread it onto a baking sheet. (The thinner the layer the better, as you are trying to cool the risotto down quickly). Put the risotto into the fridge to cool completely, then wrap the pan with plastic wrap and store for up to 2 days. When ready to serve, return the risotto to a pan with the final third of hot broth. Stir until the liquid is absorbed, and the rice is creamy.

NUTTY RICE PILAF

Serves 6

intro

Rice pilaf is an ancient dish that works extremely well in a modern, busy kitchen. This version uses tart dried cherries—readily available in markets—and chopped pecans which add to the nutty flavor of the sautéed rice. You'll find yourself making this side dish over and over again!

ingredients

2 tablespoons unsalted butter
1 small yellow onion, diced
1/2 cup chopped pecans
1/2 cup dried cherries
2 cups long-grain white rice
4 cups chicken broth
Salt and freshly ground pepper

method

In a saucepot, melt the butter. Add the onion and sauté till tender, about 5 minutes. Add the pecans and cherries and sauté briefly. Add the rice and stir to coat. Add the broth and bring to a boil. Cover the pot, reduce the heat to low, and cook for 18 minutes, or until all of the liquid is absorbed.

TOASTED RICE with PIQUILLO PEPPERS and ARTICHOKES

Serves 8

intro

I love Spanish rice for brunch or dinner buffets, since it's packed with flavor, color and spice. The artichokes and piquillo peppers, a favorite sweet Spanish pepper, add zest and the rice serves a large crowd easily.

ingredients

5 tablespoons extra-virgin oil
1 tablespoon unsalted butter
1 yellow onion, diced
2 garlic cloves, minced
1 cup sliced piquillo peppers (from a jar), drained
1 cup marinated artichoke hearts, drained and chopped
Freshly ground pepper
1 bay leaf
3 cups long grain white rice
6 cups chicken broth

method

Heat three tablespoons of olive oil in a large saucepot over medium heat. Add the rice and sauté until golden, about 3 minutes, stirring often. Remove the rice from the pan and set aside. Add the remaining two tablespoons of olive oil and the butter to the pan along with the onion and garlic and sauté until tender, about 10 minutes, stirring often. Add the piquillo peppers, artichokes and bay leaf and sauté 2 minutes more. Add the rice back to the pot. Add the chicken broth, bring the mixture to a boil, then cover the pot with a lid and reduce the heat to a simmer. Cook the rice for 20 minutes, without opening the pot or stirring, or until almost all of the liquid has evaporated.

Gently fluff the rice with a fork and serve.

CREAMY POLENTA with CRUMBLED BLUE CHEESE

Serves 6

intro

Polenta, a staple of Northern Italy started out as a "peasant" food; Today it is the ultimate comforting side dish or base for roasted or braised meats and stews. And, I love the creaminess that the blue cheese and Parmesan add to the comforting texture of the cornmeal. I serve a Barolo with the polenta, as it is the perfect Italian wine for rich flavors.

ingredients

2 cups chicken stock
2 cups whole milk
1 1/2 cups quick-cooking polenta
2 tablespoons unsalted butter
1/2 cup grated Parmesan cheese
4 ounces crumbled blue cheese
Freshly ground white pepper

method

Bring the chicken stock and milk to a boil in a saucepan. Once the liquid comes to a boil, stir in the polenta, using a whisk to remove any lumps. Cook for 1 minute. Stir in the butter and Parmesan cheese and season with white pepper. Garnish the polenta with the crumbled blue cheese.

Vegetable Side Dishes

Glazed Root Vegetables with Lemon and Honey

Brussels Sprouts with Bacon and Shallots

Cheesy Broccoli

Cauliflower Gratin

Layers and Layers of Eggplant

Spicy Parmesan Corn on the Cob

Spicy Vegetarian Chili

Red Wine Mushroom Ragout

GLAZED ROOT VEGETABLES with LEMON and HONEY

Serves 8

intro

Roasted root vegetables are so delicious and flavorful… not to mention so easy to prepare! The honey helps the natural caramelization that occurs through roasting, bringing out the sweetness in the vegetables. This side dish pairs beautifully with roasted or grilled meats.

ingredients

1 pound parsnips, peeled and cut into 1-inch pieces
1 pound carrots, peeled, cut into 1-inch pieces
1 pound rutabagas, peeled, cut into 1-inch pieces
4 tablespoons extra-virgin olive oil
1 teaspoon grated lemon zest
1/4 cup fresh lemon juice
3 tablespoons honey
Salt and freshly ground pepper
1/2 cup chopped parsley

method

Position two racks in the oven and preheat the oven to 400°F.

Combine the parsnips, carrots, rutabagas, olive oil, lemon zest, lemon juice and honey in a large mixing bowl and toss to coat. Season liberally with salt and pepper.

Divide the vegetable mixture among two baking sheets. Roast the vegetables for 30 minutes, stirring occasionally and reversing the position of the baking sheets halfway during the roasting process. Remove the pan from the oven and stir the vegetables, then return them to the oven and continue to roast for another 30 minutes, or until the vegetables are tender and caramelized.

chef's tip

To make the vegetables in advance of serving, leave them at room temperature after roasting. To rewarm, place them in a 450°F oven for 10 minutes or until heated through.

BRUSSELS SPROUTS with ROASTED SHALLOTS and BACON

Serves 8

intro

I love the natural sweetness of caramelized shallots combined with the earthiness of brussels sprouts…And who doesn't love bacon! This is another easy preparation, allowing the true flavor of the vegetables to come through in the roasting process.

ingredients

24 small shallots
2 tablespoons extra-virgin olive oil
2 pounds brussels sprouts, preferably small and uniform in size
Salt and freshly ground pepper
6 slices thick-cut applewood smoked bacon, cut into 1-inch pieces
3 tablespoons grated Parmesan cheese

method

Preheat the oven to 400°F. Peel the shallots, leaving the root ends intact, so that the shallots hold together. Place the shallots on a baking sheet, drizzle 1 tablespoon of oil over them and season liberally with salt and pepper. Place the shallots in the oven and roast for 10 minutes.

Trim the stems of the brussels sprouts and cut each brussel in half lengthwise, cutting through the stem end. Toss the brussels sprouts with the remaining tablespoon of olive oil and season with salt and pepper.

Add the brussels sprouts to the baking sheet with the shallots and continue roasting, tossing twice during cooking, until the brussel sprouts are tender and lightly browned, about 20 minutes more.

Place the bacon pieces in a sauté pan over medium heat and cook until crisp. Drain the bacon and toss the crisp bacon with the roasted shallots and brussels sprouts. Sprinkle with Parmesan cheese and serve.

CHEESY BROCCOLI

Serves 4

intro

When choosing broccoli, look for a head of broccoli with a tight, firm flower. Steaming the broccoli will give it vibrant color as well as help it to retain its nutrients and all of its wonderful flavor. And, let's face it…Cheese makes everything good!

ingredients

For the Broccoli:
2 pounds fresh broccoli
2 tablespoons unsalted butter
Pinch of salt

For the Cheese Sauce:
4 slices American cheese, diced
1 3-ounce package cream cheese, cubed
1 cup grated sharp cheddar cheese
3 tablespoons whole milk
2 dashes Tabasco

method

Trim 3 of the heavy stalk from the bottom of each broccoli flower with a sharp paring knife then split each stalk lengthwise through its stem into 3 or 4 pieces. Place the broccoli in a shallow saucepan and pour in just enough water to cover the bottom of the pan by 1/2-inch. Add the butter and salt to the pan and place the pan over medium high. Bring the water to a full boil, place a tight-fitting lid over the pan and steam the broccoli until just tender, about 5 minutes.

Combine the three cheeses in the bowl of a food processor fitted with a steel blade. Add in the milk and Tabasco. Run the food processor until the mixture becomes a smooth sauce, about 2 to 3 minutes.

Place the cheese topping in a small saucepan and heat over low heat, stirring constantly, for 3 minutes or until the sauce is melted and smooth.

To serve, drain the liquid from the saucepan and arrange the steamed broccoli in a casserole or serving bowl. Pour the melted cheese sauce over the broccoli.

CAULIFLOWER GRATIN

Serves 8

intro

Cauliflower is a wonderfully hearty vegetable and adding the savory blend of Gruyere and Parmesan, with a little Panko for texture, makes this dish a true crowd pleaser.

ingredients

1 large head cauliflower, cut into large florets
2 cups heavy cream
1 cup freshly grated Gruyere
1/2 cup freshly grated Parmesan
1/4 teaspoon grated nutmeg
1/4 cup Panko crumbs (Japanese bread crumbs)
Salt and freshly ground pepper

method

Preheat the oven to 375°F.

Place two inches of water in the bottom of a high-sided sauté pan. Bring the water to a boil. Add the cauliflower florets and steam for 4 minutes, or until the cauliflower is tender but still firm. Drain the cauliflower and set it aside.

Pour the cream into a medium-sized saucepan and place it over medium heat. Bring the cream to a boil, reduce the heat to a simmer and add the Gruyere and Parmesan cheeses, whisking to melt the cheeses and make a smooth sauce. Remove the sauce from the heat and season with nutmeg, salt and pepper.

Pour one third of the sauce into the bottom of a casserole or baking dish. Pile the drained cauliflower on top, then pour the rest of the sauce evenly over the top. Sprinkle the Panko crumbs over the top of the casserole. Bake for 20 minutes or until the sauce is bubbling and browned on top. Serve hot or at room temperature.

LAYERS and LAYERS of EGGPLANT, TOMATO and MOZZARELLA

Serves 6

intro

This is my version of the classic Italian Eggplant Parmesan. When buying eggplants, look for medium-size ones, as larger eggplants tend to be watery and bitter. A great dish for a busy night, this also works beautifully for a vegetarian meal, served with a crisp green salad and toasted garlic bread.

ingredients

2 large eggplants
1 cup all purpose flour
1/2 teaspoon dried oregano
3 cups marinara sauce
2 teaspoons dried oregano
About 1 cup extra-virgin olive oil
1 cup grated Parmesan Cheese
2 cups shredded mozzarella cheese
10 fresh basil leaves, cut into thin strips

method

Preheat the oven to 375°F.

Slice the eggplant into 1/4-inch slices. Combine the flour and oregano in a shallow bowl and season it with salt and pepper. Dredge each slice of eggplant in the flour and shake off any excess. Heat 1/2-inch of olive oil in a large sauté pan over medium-high heat. Sauté the eggplant, in batches, until deep golden brown in color. Drain the eggplant on paper towels.

Combine the mozzarella and Parmesan cheeses in a mixing bowl.

Using a 3-quart baking dish, spread 1 cup of marinara sauce onto the bottom of the casserole. Layer one-third of the eggplant slices to cover the sauce. Sprinkle the eggplant with one-third of the cheese mixture, then sprinkle with a couple of tablespoons of the basil. Repeat the layering process two times, ending with the cheese.

Bake the casserole for 25 minutes, or until golden brown and bubbling on top. Let cool slightly before serving.

SPICY PARMESAN
CORN on the COB

Serves 6

intro

Corn is such a versatile vegetable, lending its flavor to so many of the world's cuisines. My spicy parmesan corn on the cob has a little bit of Mexico and a little bit of Italy—a great marriage of flavors! The jalapeño in the cooking water adds heat, while the butter and parmesan coat every kernel for rich cheesy flavor. Make plenty, as your guests will ask for seconds!

ingredients

16 cups water
2 fresh jalapeños, split in half
6 ears of corn, shucked and cleaned
3 cups grated cups grated Parmesan cheese
1 tablespoon freshly ground pepper
1 stick unsalted butter, melted

method

Place the water in a stockpot and add the jalapeños.   Bring the water to a boil, reduce the heat and simmer for 3 minutes. Bring the water back up to a boil, add the ears of corn and cook the corn for 10 minutes.

Combine the Parmesan cheese and ground pepper in a shallow casserole dish, large enough to hold one ear of corn at a time. Melt the butter in another shallow casserole dish and set up an assembly line starting with the pot of corn, then the butter and the cheese.

Remove one ear of corn from the water, place it in the melted butter and roll to coat, then place the buttered ear of corn into the cheese and coat well. Repeat using the remaining ears of corn.

SPICY VEGETARIAN CHILI

Serves 6 to 8

intro

Break out your soup pot and fix up a batch of this delicious, spicy vegetarian chili. Using three different beans, three different peppers and the convenience of canned chilies and tomatoes, this spicy chili is a one-pot masterpiece! Sour cream and fresh chopped cilantro are perfect condiments. Serve with freshly baked cornbread or tortillas warm from the oven.

ingredients

2 tablespoons olive oil
1 small yellow onion, diced
1 red bell pepper, cleaned and diced
1 green or yellow bell pepper, cleaned and diced
1/2 jalapeño pepper, seeds and veins removed and minced
3 garlic cloves, minced
Two 4-ounce cans chopped green chiles
3 tablespoons chili powder
1 bay leaf
1 teaspoon ground cumin
1 tablespoon dried oregano
Salt
One 28-ounce can crushed tomatoes in juice
One 14.5-ounce can crushed tomatoes
One 15-ounce can kidney beans, drained
One 15-ounce can garbanzo beans, drained
One 15-ounce can black beans
One 15-ounce can whole kernel corn
Grated Cheddar cheese, for garnish
Sour cream, for garnish

method

Heat the olive oil in a large pot over medium heat. Add the onion and sauté until caramelized and tender, about 15 minutes, stirring often. Add the bell peppers, jalapeño, garlic and green chiles and sauté 5 minutes longer. Add the chili powder, bay leaf, cumin and oregano and season with salt. Add the diced and crushed tomatoes to the pot along with the kidney beans, garbanzo beans and black beans. Bring the chili to a boil, reduce the heat to low, and simmer for 45 minutes. Stir in the corn and continue cooking 5 minutes more. Serve piping hot bowls of chili with cheddar cheese and dollops of sour cream.

RED WINE MUSHROOM RAGOUT

Serves 6 as an appetizer

intro

Simple, sophisticated and scrumptious. I like to serve these mushrooms on slices of crunchy French baguette as an appetizer and I serve my steaks smothered in the ragout, then drizzled with truffle oil for that fabulously fragrant effect. Or spoon the mushroom ragout over a scoop of garlic mashed potatoes in a martini glass for an easy to eat buffet treat. Try using criminis, shitakes, oyster mushrooms, button mushrooms….or a mix of domestic and exotics.

ingredients

2 tablespoons unsalted butter
2 tablespoons extra-virgin olive oil
2 large shallots, minced
2 garlic cloves, minced
4 cups mixed mushrooms, sliced
2 teaspoons fresh thyme leaves
2 tablespoons fresh chives, chopped
Salt & freshly ground pepper

method

Combine the butter and oil in a large skillet. Add the shallots and garlic and cook over low heat until translucent, about 5 minutes. Add the mushrooms and thyme, season with salt and pepper and sauté over medium-high heat, stirring often, until the mushroom liquid has evaporated, about 10 minutes. Serve warm or at room temperature, garnished with chives.

A Delicious Dessert Buffet

Butterscotch Pudding

Southern Bread Pudding with Brandy Sauce

Cherries Jubilee

Bananas Foster

Brown Sugar Apple Cobbler

Biscotti Stuffed Baked Apples

Berry Grunt

Summer Peach Cobbler

The Ultimate Bittersweet Hot Fudge Sauce

Red Wine Poached Pears
with Brown Sugar Cream

BUTTERSCOTCH PUDDING

Serves 6 to 8

intro

With a dollop of whipped cream on top, this rich and creamy pudding is the perfect ending to any meal. My caramel-colored, toffee-flavored butterscotch pudding is a great partner to dark chocolate brownies...Try a dollop of whipped cream on top of the pudding, on top of the brownie, all topped with a sprinkling of gingersnap cookie crumbs, and you have the ultimate dessert!

ingredients

2 1/4 cups whole milk
1 cup heavy whipping cream
6 tablespoons unsalted butter
1 1/4 cups light brown sugar
3 egg yolks
1/4 cup cornstarch
1 teaspoon pure vanilla extract
Pinch of salt

method

In a large saucepan, combine the milk and cream and bring to a simmer over medium heat. Once the mixture comes to a full simmer, remove the pan from the heat and set it aside.

In a large sauté pan, melt the butter over medium heat. Stir in the brown sugar and cook 5 minutes, stirring constantly, to caramelize the mixture. Once the butter browns, and the aroma becomes sweet and nutty, remove the pan from the heat and gradually add the butter/sugar mixture to the milk/cream mixture.

continued on next page

BUTTERSCOTCH PUDDING

Continued

Place the egg yolks in a small bowl and whisk in 1/2 cup of the hot milk mixture, to temper the egg yolks and keep them from scrambling. Whisk the egg mixture back into the hot milk mixture in the saucepan. Add the cornstarch and salt to the pan and place the pan over medium heat. Bring the mixture to a simmer, whisking constantly, until the pudding is thick, about 2 minutes. Remove the pan from the heat and stir in the vanilla extract. Serve the pudding warm, or ladle the pudding into ramekins and refrigerate until set.

Serve garnished with a dollop of whipped cream on each serving.

chef's tip

Tempering gradually brings the temperature of two mixtures together and is used when a scalding hot liquid, such as cream or milk, is added to eggs. The method is usually used for puddings and custards, crème brulee and pastry cream.

SOUTHERN BREAD PUDDING with BRANDY SAUCE

Serves 6

intro

Food historians have found references to bread pudding through the ages, including recipes in ancient Egypt for bread puddings with cream, raisins and almonds and from ancient India with rosewater and saffron-flavored syrup. This bread pudding has its roots in the American South and features a rich Caramel Brandy Sauce. Use quality French bread and be sure to allow the bread to soak up all of the custard before baking.

ingredients

1/2 cup golden raisins
1/3 cup Brandy
1 1/2 cups whole milk
1 cup heavy whipping cream
3/4 cup granulated sugar
3 whole eggs
2 egg yolks
1 teaspoon pure vanilla extract
1/4 teaspoon ground cinnamon
12 ounces French bread, cut into 1-inch cubes

Caramel Brandy Sauce:
2 cups heavy cream
1/2 cup granulated white sugar
2 tablespoons cornstarch
1/2 cup Brandy
2 tablespoons unsalted butter

Method

Preheat the oven to 375°F.

Combine the raisins and Brandy in a non-reactive bowl and let soak for 30 minutes. Drain the raisins, reserving the Brandy, and set both aside.

continued on next page

SOUTHERN BREAD PUDDING with BRANDY SAUCE

Continued

In a large mixing bowl, whisk together the milk, sugar, heavy cream, eggs, vanilla and cinnamon. Add the French bread pieces, raisins and reserved Brandy. Stir to combine, then let the mixture sit at room temperature for 30 minutes, to allow the bread to soak up the liquid. Pour the mixture into a 3-quart casserole or a baking dish. Cover the pan with a lid or aluminum foil and bake for 40 minutes. Remove the foil and bake for an additional 20 minutes, or until the top of the bread pudding is puffed and golden.

For the sauce, combine the cream and sugar in a saucepot and bring to a simmer over medium heat, stirring to dissolve the sugar. Place the cornstarch and 1/4 cup of the Brandy in a small mixing bowl and whisk to make a slurry. (A slurry is a paste that acts as a thickener when stirred into hot soups, stews and sauces.) Pour the slurry into the cream mixture and simmer the sauce, stirring constantly, until it thickens, about 3 minutes. Remove the sauce from the heat and stir in the butter and the remaining 1/4 cup of the Brandy.

Serve the sauce with the warm bread pudding.

CHERRIES JUBILEE

Serves 6

intro

A "jubilee" is an occasion of a joyful celebration, and that is exactly what you create when you offer your guests a dessert of Cherries Jubilee. This final course is a show (igniting the fruit at the table always seems to thrill guests!), perfect prepared tableside or made in advance and offered on a dessert buffet. Serve these sweet and succulent cherries at your next dinner party to restore nostalgic memories.

ingredients

16 ounces canned, pitted sour cherries, with their juice
1/2 cup granulated sugar
2 tablespoons grated orange zest
1 tablespoon cornstarch or arrowroot
1/3 cup Kirsch or Cognac
1 pint vanilla ice cream
Chocolate shavings, for garnish

method

Drain the cherries, reserving the juice. Measure the juice and add enough water to measure 1 1/2 cups of liquid. Pour the liquid into a small saucepan and add the sugar and orange zest. Bring the mixture to a boil, reduce the heat and simmer, uncovered, for 10 minutes.

Place the arrowroot in a small mixing bowl. Remove 2 tablespoons of the cherry liquid from the pot and add it to the arrowroot. Stir the mixture to dissolve. Gradually stir the arrowroot mixture into the liquid in the pan. Simmer, stirring constantly until thick, about 2 minutes. Add the cherries and stir to combine.

Remove the pan from the heat and add the Kirsch. Use a long match or automatic flame to ignite the mixture. Gently stir the mixture until the flame dies down.

Divide the ice cream among six bowls. Spoon the sauce over the ice cream and garnish with the chocolate shavings.

BANANAS FOSTER

Serves 6

intro

The historical New Orleans' restaurant Brennan's claims the invention of Bananas Foster. In the 1950s, New Orleans was the major port of entry for bananas shipped from Central and South America and restaurant owner Owen Brennan challenged his chef to make something interesting with the fruit. Bananas Foster was an immediate hit and Brennan's continues to serve tens of thousands of pounds of it each year. In my house, Bananas Foster also doubles as a perfect topping for French Toast!

ingredients

1 stick unsalted butter
1 cup dark brown sugar
6 small bananas, peeled, sliced lengthwise and halved
1/2 cup banana liqueur or dark Rum
1/2 teaspoon ground cinnamon

method

Melt the butter in a large skillet over medium-low heat. Add the brown sugar and cook the mixture until the sugar dissolves, about 3 minutes. Add the bananas and cook for 2 minutes on each side, until just tender, turning once. Remove the pan from the heat and add the banana liqueur or Rum, along with the cinnamon, to the pan and carefully ignite the alcohol using a long match or automatic flame. Place the pan back on the stove and simmer the mixture until the flame dies out. Serve the Bananas Foster over ice cream.

BROWN SUGAR APPLE COBBLER

Serves 6 to 8

intro

The variety of apples in this cobbler creates a medley of hard-to-resist sweet and tangy flavors. Baked together with butter, brown sugar and a streusel topping, this is true comfort food!

ingredients

4 tablespoons unsalted butter
1 cup firmly packed light brown sugar
2 tablespoons freshly grated lemon zest
2 tablespoons fresh lemon juice
2 tablespoons all-purpose flour
2 pounds Granny Smith apples, cored, peeled and sliced 1/4-inch thick
2 pounds McIntosh or Gala apples, cored, peeled and sliced 1/4-inch thick
2 ounces Calvados
1/2 teaspoon ground cinnamon
Pinch of salt

Streusel Topping:
1/2 cup granulated sugar
1/2 cup brown sugar
1 cup all-purpose flour
1/2 cup chopped pecans
2 teaspoons cinnamon
1 1/2 sticks unsalted butter, cut into small cubes and kept cold
Whipped cream, for garnish

method

Preheat the oven to 375°F.

In a large skillet, melt 3 tablespoons of the butter over medium-high heat. Add the brown sugar, lemon juice and the flour. Stir the mixture for 1 minute to dissolve the sugar. Add the apples and cook, stirring often, for 5 minutes. Remove the pan from the heat and add the Calvados. Return the pan to the heat and cook for 2 minutes more. Remove the pan from the heat and stir in the cinnamon and salt.

continued on next page

BROWN SUGAR APPLE COBBLER

Continued

In a large mixing bowl, combine the sugars, flour, pecans, cinnamon, salt and butter. Blend the mixture well with your hands or use a pastry cutter, until the streusel resembles coarse crumbs.

Top the apples with the streusel and bake until the top is lightly browned, about 45 minutes.

chef's tip

To make cutting the butter into the flour/sugar mixture a bit easier, try grating a frozen stick of butter on the large holes of a box grater. You'll have small bits of cold butter which will help the coarse meal come together quickly! And, use a melon baller to scoop out the core of the apple halves quickly and with minimal waste.

BISCOTTI STUFFED BAKED APPLES

Serves 6

intro

This biscotti stuffing adds great crunch to baked apples and the tart dried cherries add tang and color. A little bit like a deconstructed apple-cherry pie, all the familiar flavors of cinnamon, butter and honey are packed into pretty apple packages. Easy to make, stuffed baked apples will make you a hero to kids and adults alike!

ingredients

- **2 tablespoons Calvados or apple juice**
- **1/2 cup dried cherries**
- **3 tablespoons honey**
- **2 almond biscotti cookies**
- **6 Rome apples or other baking apples**
- **3 tablespoons unsalted butter**
- **6 whole cinnamon sticks**

method

Preheat the oven to 350°F.

In a small mixing bowl combine the Calvados or apple juice, dried cherries, and honey. Place the biscotti in a sealable plastic bag and use a rolling pin or the bottom of a small sauté pan to crush the cookies into small pieces. Add the broken cookies to the fruit mixture and set the stuffing aside.

Cut about a 1/2-inch slice off the top of each apple. (The apple tops are perfect for snacking.) Scoop out the seeds of the apple, using a melon baller or a small teaspoon, to make a pocket. Pack 2 tablespoons of the stuffing into each of the apples. Top each apple with a teaspoon of the butter. Place a cinnamon stick into the center of each apple, to resemble a stem.

Set the stuffed apples into a 3-quart casserole or baking dish. Pour the remaining Calvados or apple juice into the pan. Bake the apples for 45 minutes or until they are tender when a small sharp knife is inserted and the top is golden browned.

BERRY GRUNT

Serves 6

intro

A "Grunt" is a dumpling-topped fruit dessert, cooked on top of the stove. Berry grunts are a traditional favorite in the northeast and they acquired their unusual name because a tightly-covered skillet will "grunt" while the dessert steams. Here, blackberries and raspberries simmer together, then dollops of ginger-spiked dumpling batter are added to the pan, to steam in berry juice….Delicious!

ingredients

1 1/2 cups granulated sugar
1/2 teaspoon ground cinnamon
3/4 cup all-purpose flour
3/4 teaspoon baking powder
Pinch of salt
1/4 teaspoon ground ginger
1/3 cup whole milk, at room temperature
2 tablespoons unsalted butter, melted
4 cups raspberries
4 cups blackberries
2 tablespoons fresh lemon juice
Whipped cream, for garnish

method

Stir together 2 tablespoons of sugar and 1/2 teaspoon cinnamon in a small bowl and set it aside. In a mixing bowl, whisk together the flour, 1/4 cup sugar, baking powder, salt, and the ginger in a medium bowl. Add the milk and melted butter and stir to combine. Set the batter aside.

Combine the raspberries, blackberries, lemon juice, remaining 1 1/2 cups sugar, a pinch of salt and 2 tablespoons water in a 3-quart pot. Place the pot over medium heat on top of the stove and bring the mixture to a boil. Reduce the heat and simmer to dissolve the sugar, about 2 minutes.

Drop 6 large dollops of the batter on top of the berry mixture, spacing them evenly. Sprinkle the dumplings with the cinnamon-sugar mixture. Cover the pot and cook the Grunt over medium-low heat until the dumplings are cooked through, about 15 minutes. Serve warm, topped with whipped cream.

SUMMER PEACH COBBLER

Serves 6

intro

Peaches open the door to summer! As soon as you see beautiful ripe peaches
appearing in the farm stands, gather up the ingredients for this seasonal favorite.
In the true Southern Style, my Summer Peach Cobbler is bursting with juicy fruit and
fabulous flavor.

ingredients

8 ripe peaches, peeled and sliced (about 6 cups)
1 1/2 cups granulated sugar
1 teaspoon ground ginger
1/2 cup water
4 tablespoons butter, melted
3/4 cups self-rising flour
3/4 cup whole milk
1 teaspoon vanilla
Pinch of salt
Whipped cream, for garnish

method

Preheat the oven to 350°F.

Combine the peaches, 1 cup of the sugar, ginger and water in a saucepan. Bring the
mixture to a boil, then reduce the heat and simmer for 10 minutes.

Pour the melted butter into a 3-quart casserole or deep baking dish.

In a mixing bowl whisk together the remaining 1/2 cup sugar, flour, milk, vanilla and salt.
Blend until well combined and no clumps exist. Pour the batter over the melted butter in
the baking dish and DO NOT STIR. Spoon the peaches on top of the batter, gently
pouring in the syrup. (The batter will rise to the top during baking). Bake for
40 to 45 minutes, or until golden and puffed.

Serve with a big dollop of whipped cream on each serving.

THE ULTIMATE BITTERSWEET HOT FUDGE SAUCE

Serves 8

intro

If you're a chocolate lover—and love the true taste of dark, bittersweet chocolate—then this sauce is for you. Serve this silky chocolate decadence over cream puffs, ice cream, waffles (for an indulgent breakfast treat!) or on a sundae bar with lots of ice cream toppings.

ingredients

1 pound high-quality bittersweet chocolate, chopped
1 stick plus 3 tablespoons unsalted butter, at room temperature
1 cup granulated sugar
1 cup heavy cream
1/2 cup hot water
2 teaspoons vanilla extract
Pinch of salt

method

Combine the chocolate, butter, sugar, cream and water in the top of a double boiler. Melt the mixture, over simmering water, on medium-low heat. Remove from the heat and stir in the vanilla and salt. Serve or bottle.

RED WINE POACHED PEARS
with BROWN SUGAR CREAM

Serves 8

intro

This red wine poaching liquid turns the pears a deep berry color to create a stunning dessert. Vanilla and clove compliment the brown sugar sour cream and when topped with a sprinkle of toasted pistachios, this dish is always impressive.

ingredients

1 cup dry red wine
1 cup Port
1 cup water
3/4 cup granulated sugar
4 whole cloves
4 2-inch by 1-inch strips of lemon peel
1 vanilla bean, split lengthwise
4 firm Bosc pears, halved and cored
1 cup sour cream
2 tablespoons brown sugar
Toasted pistachios, for garnish

method

Combine the red wine, Port, sugar, cloves, lemon peel and vanilla bean in a large saucepot. Add the pear halves, cut side down and bring the mixture to a simmer over medium-low heat. Simmer until the pears are tender, about 10 minutes. Using a slotted spoon, transfer the pears to a plate. Increase the heat to medium-high and boil the poaching liquid until it is reduced to 3/4 cup, about 10 minutes. Remove the pan from heat and cool the sauce.

In a mixing bowl whisk together the sour cream and brown sugar.

To serve, pour a pool of the reduced poaching liquid onto 8 dessert plates. Place 1 pear half, cut side up, on each plate. Fill the cavity of each pear half with two tablespoons of the brown sugar sour cream, garnish with pistachios and serve.

Cheers To You!

Double Dark Hot Chocolate

Café Brulot

Mulled Wine

Cranberry Apple Cider

Hot Buttered Run

Holiday Eggnog

DOUBLE DARK HOT CHOCOLATE

Serves 8

intro

Infuse your favorite flavoring into this rich, creamy hot chocolate by adding a couple of drops of peppermint oil or orange oil (available in gourmet food stores) or by spiking the cocoa with your favorite liqueur. I use peppermint schnapps at the holidays, Kahlua on cold nights and Amaretto or Chambord when I want bold flavor.

ingredients

6 cups whole milk
2 cups half and half
1/2 cup high-quality Dutch process cocoa powder
4 ounces bittersweet chocolate, chips or chopped
1 cup granulated sugar
1 teaspoon vanilla extract
Lots of mini marshmallows

method

Combine the milk and half and half in a saucepan and bring to a simmer over medium heat.

In a small mixing bowl, combine the cocoa powder, chopped chocolate and sugar. Add a few teaspoons of the hot milk mixture to the cocoa mixture and blend to make a paste. Scrape the paste into the saucepan with the remaining milk mixture and whisk until smooth. Simmer for 2 minutes.

To avoid scorching, do not let the mixture come to a boil. Remove the saucepan from the heat, stir in the vanilla and serve topped with lots of marshmallows.

CAFÉ BRULOT

Serves 6

intro

You will literally "light up the table" with this flaming coffee drink! Cafe Brulot has long been a favorite New Orleans treat, served as a festive after-dinner digestive at New Orleans restaurants. Those who take their coffee and/or cocktails seriously have also been known to serve it at breakfast or brunch, referring to it as an "eye opener." This recipe is my favorite version of the classic and is especially beautiful served in clear glass mugs or goblets, with a dollop of whipped cream on top.

ingredients

Peel of 1 orange, cut into 1 by 1/8-inch strips
Peel of 1 lemon, cut into 1 by 1/8-inch strips
6 tablespoons granulated sugar
2 cups Cognac or Kahlua
1 cup Grand Marnier or Cointreau
4 cups fresh dark roast coffee

method

Combine the orange peel, lemon peel, sugar cubes, Cognac and Grand Marnier in a saucepot and place over medium-low heat.   Stir to dissolve the sugar. When the mixture is warm, remove the pan from the heat and ignite the alcohol with a long match or an automatic flame. Stirring gently, pour the coffee into the pot in a slow, thin stream, continuing to stir until the flame dies out. Ladle into cups and serve at once.

MULLED WINE

Serves 8

Known as glögg in Nordic countries, it is also called vin brulé or "burnt wine" in France, quentão or "big hot" in Brazil, and vin fiert or "boiled wine" in Romania. The heat releases the perfume of the wine and spices, making it the perfect warm drink for chilly weather!

ingredients

One 750-ml bottle dry red wine, such as Cabernet Sauvignon or Zinfandel
1 cup granulated sugar
Zest of 1 orange
6 cloves
2 cinnamon sticks
One 1-inch piece fresh ginger, peeled and sliced
1 cup Brandy
1/2 cup golden raisins
1/2 cup slivered almonds
Long cinnamon sticks, for stirring

method

Combine the red wine, sugar, orange zest, cloves, cinnamon sticks and ginger in a saucepot and place over medium heat. Stir until the sugar dissolves and the wine is hot, but do not boil. Pour in the Brandy and let the mixture sit over low heat for 5 minutes to incorporate the flavors.

Serve warm, with raisins and almonds for guests to add to their drinks, as desired.

CRANBERRY APPLE CIDER

Serves 8

intro

This non-alcoholic hot blend of cranberry juice and apple cider infused with brown sugar and holiday spices is something you can keep warming on the stove all day for guests. The hot cider fills your home with the aroma of the holidays and the fresh ginger adds a hint of spicy flavor.

ingredients

8 cups apple cider
2 cups cranberry juice
1/4 cup packed brown sugar
2 cinnamon sticks
10 whole cloves
1 orange, peeled and sliced
One 2-inch piece of fresh ginger, peeled and sliced

method

Combine the apple cider, cranberry juice, brown sugar, cinnamon sticks, cloves, orange slices and ginger in a saucepot. Bring the mixture to a simmer over medium heat, then reduce the heat to a simmer. Simmer for 15 minutes, then strain and serve.

HOT BUTTERED RUM

Serves 8

intro

Use the freshest spices and unsalted, sweet butter for a holiday tradition that will last for years to come.

ingredients

1 1/2 cups packed dark brown sugar
2 sticks unsalted butter, room temperature
1/2 cup honey
1 teaspoon ground cinnamon
1/2 teaspoon ground nutmeg
1/8 teaspoon ground cloves
Pinch of salt
1 1/2 cups Spiced Rum
4 cups boiling water
4 cinnamon sticks

method

Using an electric mixer beat the brown sugar, butter, honey, cinnamon, nutmeg, cloves and salt until blended and smooth. Transfer the mixture to a 3-quart saucepot. Place the pot over medium heat and add the Rum and the boiling water. Stir until the butter dissolves and the mixture is heated through, but do not boil. Garnish with the cinnamon sticks and serve.

HOLIDAY EGG NOG

Serves 8

intro

Freshly ground nutmeg and a healthy amount of Rum make this Eggnog the favorite drink for holiday brunches, tree trimming parties and time by the fire.

ingredients

5 cups whole milk
6 eggs, slightly beaten
2/3 cup granulated sugar
Pinch of salt
2 teaspoons vanilla extract
1 cup Rum
2 cups heavy whipping cream
Ground nutmeg, for garnish

method

Combine the milk, eggs, sugar and salt in a 3-quart saucepan. Cook over low heat for 15 to 20 minutes, stirring constantly, until the mixture coats the back of a spoon. Remove from heat and stir in the vanilla and rum.

Using an electric mixer, beat the cream until stiff peaks form. Gently stir 2 cups of the whipped cream into the eggnog mixture. Drop spoonfuls of the remaining whipped cream in mounds onto the eggnog. Sprinkle with nutmeg and serve.

BUFFET BASICS

BUFFET BASICS

Buffets are a wonderful way to host a party and still enjoy time with family and friends, without getting caught up in the kitchen or serving the meal. And, as the host, a menu that is offered buffet-style allows you time to mingle and enjoy! Whether its a sumptuous Spring Buffet, a Summer bash, a Fall Pot Luck or a hearty Winter feast, your guests will be delighted by the wide array of delicious dishes for every season.

In addition to providing a practical way to serve a large group of people, a beautiful, abundant buffet adds a celebratory focal point to any event. Everyone loves an Italian Buffet, with a trio of pastas to choose from. A Dessert Buffet is a romantic way to rejoice with friends at the end of a get-together. And an easy, informal buffet ensures that everyone, hosts and guests alike, can enjoy a home cooked meal and a night filled with great conversation. Organize your next buffet around a theme or holiday and keep in mind that guests have only one hand to work with while going through the buffet line, so be sure to provide lots of serving utensils and sauces or garnishes in close proximity to your delicious dishes.

For stress-free entertaining, follow my "Party Guidelines":

- *Plan for 3 drinks per guest and buy enough ice to provide 1 pound of ice per person (this allows for melting!)*

- *To determine how much liquor you will need, keep in mind that there are six glasses in a standard-size bottle of wine or Champagne*

- *Count on 4 to 6 hors d'oeuvres per person if you're serving a meal. If you're only serving cocktails and hors d'oeuvres, plan on guests eating 10 to 12 tastes per person*

- *A portion of meat per person is about 1/4 to 1/3 of a pound*

- *The perfect portion of vegetables, rice, pasta or salad is about 1/2 cup*

- *Don't forget the vegetarians!*

BUFFET BASICS

PRESENTATION IS EVERYTHING!

ARTICHOKE VOTIVES
Looking to create a decorative buffet table or dinner table? Try making vegetable creations to jazz up your display. Separate the petals of a raw artichoke, and with scissors, cut out the tender center petals until you reach the choke (fuzzy center). Squeeze a few drops of lemon juice into the hole to prevent the inner petals from turning brown. Insert a glass votive and drop in a tea light candle. Refrigerate until ready to use, to keep the artichoke from oxidizing.

CREATIVE COCKTAILS
Create elegant cocktails by making glamorous ice cubes! Freeze strawberries or raspberries in ice cubes and float one or two cubes in each cocktail for a dazzling drink.

SHEER ELEGANCE
Bring your buffet table to life by transforming it from a flat, empty space. Add height by using vases filled with tall floral displays or add candles of different heights to add light and dimension. To create height for food platters, make risers using empty boxes or books of different heights, and drape a large tablecloth over the risers, bundling it in places, to cover the risers completely.

Conversion Charts

Weights and measures have been rounded up or down slightly to make measuring easier.

Volume Equivalents:

American	Metric	Imperial
1 teaspoon	5 ml	
1 tablespoon	15 ml	
1/4 cup	60 ml	2 fl.oz.
1/3 cup	75 ml	2 1/2 fl.oz.
1/2 cup	125 ml	4 fl.oz.
2/3 cup	150 ml	5 fl.oz. (1/4 pint)
3/4 cup	175 ml	6 fl.oz
1 cup	250 ml	8 fl.oz

Oven Temperatures:

225°F	(110°C) Gas 1/4
250°F	(120°C) Gas 1/2
275°F	(140°C) Gas 1
300°F	(150°C) Gas 2
325°F	(160°C) Gas 3
350°F	(180°C) Gas 4
375°F	(190°C) Gas 5
400°F	(200°C) Gas 6
425°F	(220°C) Gas 7
450°F	(230°C) Gas 8
475°F	(240°C) Gas 9

Weight Equivalents:

Imperial	Metric
1 oz.	25 g
2 oz.	50 g
3 oz.	75 g
4 oz.	125 g
5 oz.	150 g
6 oz.	175 g
7 oz.	200 g
8 oz. (1/2 lb.)	250 g
9 oz.	275 g
10 oz.	300 g
11 oz.	325 g
12 oz.	375 g
13 oz.	400 g
14 oz.	425 g
15 oz.	475 g
16 oz. (1 lb)	500 g
2 lb.	1 kg

Measurements:

Inches	CM
1/4 inch	5 mm
1/2 inch	1 cm
3/4 inch	1.5 cm
1 inch	2.5 cm
2 inches	5 cm
3 inches	7 cm
4 inches	10 cm
5 inches	12 cm
6 inches	15 cm
7 inches	18 cm
8 inches	20 cm
9 inches	23 cm
10 inches	25 cm
11 inches	28 cm
12 inches	30 cm

INDEX